A M E R I C A N

P R O F I L E S

AVIATORS

■

Robert A. Rosenbaum

Facts On File
New York • Oxford

For Gideon, taking off

Aviators

Quotations from *The Spirit of St. Louis* by Charles A. Lindbergh are reprinted with permission of Charles Scribner's Sons, an imprint of Macmillan Publishing Company. Copyright 1953 Charles Scribner's Sons; copyright renewed © 1981 Anne Morrow Lindbergh.

Facts On File, Inc.
460 Park Avenue South
New York NY 10016
USA

Facts On File Limited
c/o Roundhouse Publishing
P.O. Box 140
Oxford OX2 7SF
United Kingdom

Library of Congress Cataloging-in-Publication Data
Rosenbaum, Robert A., 1926–
    Aviators / by Robert A. Rosenbaum
        p.   cm. — (American profiles)
    Includes bibliographical references and index.
    Summary: Profiles the lives and achievements of nine pioneers in
American aviation, including the Wright brothers, Glenn Curtiss,
Charles Lindbergh, Amelia Earhart, and Chuck Yeager.
    ISBN 0-8160-2539-8
        1. Air pilots—United States—Bibliography—Juvenile literature.
[1. Air pilots.] I. Title. II. Series: American profiles (Facts
On File, Inc.)
TL539.R639   1992
629.13'092'273—dc20
[B]   91-44723

Facts On File books are available at special discounts when purchased in bulk quantities for businesses, associations, institutions or sales promotions. Please contact our Special Sales Department in New York at 212/683-2244 (dial 800/322-8755 except in NY, AK or HI) or in Oxford at 865/728399.

Jacket and text design by Ron Monteleone
Composition by Facts On File, Inc./Grace M. Ferrara
Manufactured by the Maple-Vail Book Manufacturing Group
Printed in the United States of America

10 9 8 7 6 5 4 3 2 1

This book is printed on acid-free paper.

Contents

Introduction

The eight lives profiled in this volume span the first 44 years of the history of aviation in America—from the invention of the airplane in 1903 to the breaking of the sound barrier in 1947. These were pioneering years, when the airplane developed from a curiosity to a major instrument of war and commerce, and finally to a vehicle capable of carrying humans to the threshold of space. From the historian's viewpoint, it was a very short period—so short, in fact, that one of the inventors of the airplane, Orville Wright, lived to see the breaking of the sound barrier.

Powered, heavier-than-air flying machines were the inevitable result of the combination of the internal-combustion engine and the kites and gliders with which would-be "birdmen" had been experimenting for years. The experimenters knew that air was a fluid analogous to water, capable of supporting winged craft as it already supported balloons and dirigibles. They recognized the propeller as an airscrew analogous to the screw propellers that drove steamships. Propellers had long been familiar as toys, and recently they had been successfully employed to drive airships. And of course the possibility of mounting a small internal-combustion engine—the kind that already powered automobiles and motorcycles—on a kite or glider to turn a propeller was obvious to all.

But before that could be done, experimenters had to learn how to control a craft in flight. Horizontal and vertical rudders, they reasoned, should enable fliers to steer their machines up or down, right or left. The great problem was to control lateral roll—to prevent it in straight flight, to induce it in turning. This key problem was solved by the Wright brothers with their technique of "wing warping." A few years later, a better solution was found by Glenn Curtiss with the development of the aileron. After that, aviation literally took off.

The first airplanes were propeller-driven, passenger-carrying kites. The pilot sat in the open air amid a framework of wooden slats and between two cloth-covered wings. Behind him, a small engine turned a pusher propeller. Later, the engine and propeller were placed in front of the pilot, creating the so-called "tractor

Smithsonian Institution has published on this subject, and if possible a list of other works in print in the English language."

The writer went on to explain: "I am an enthusiast, but not a crank in the sense that I have some pet theories as to the proper construction of a flying machine. I wish to avail myself of all that is already known and then if possible add my mite to help on the future worker who will attain final success."

The letter, written on the stationery of the Wright Cycle Company of Dayton, Ohio, was dated May 30, 1899. It was signed "Wilbur Wright."

In 1899, Dayton, 55 miles north of Cincinnati on the Miami River, was a thriving manufacturing center with a population of 85,000. It boasted a new 11-story skyscraper. All the streets in the center of town had recently been paved. In 1896 a local mechanic had built and operated the first automobile ever seen in the town.

Dayton's west side was a modest working-class community. At 7 Hawthorn Street, in a two-story white frame house wedged into a narrow lot, lived Milton Wright, his two sons, Wilbur and Orville, and his daughter, Katharine. Two older sons had married and moved away. His wife had died in 1889.

Milton Wright was a bishop of the Church of the United Brethren in Christ, a Protestant sect that had grown up on the midwestern frontier during the 19th century. In 1899 he was 71 years old, white-bearded and clear-eyed, with firm principles and a deep attachment to his three unmarried children.

Wilbur, born on April 16, 1867, was 32, a thin, athletic man five feet ten inches tall, confident and outgoing. His lean, clean-shaven face was dominated by a high forehead, a long nose, and piercing blue-gray eyes.

Orville, born on August 19, 1871, was 28 in 1899. Slightly shorter and heavier than his older brother, he had fine, regular features, wore a mustache, and dressed fastidiously. He was excitable and impulsive but painfully shy outside the family circle.

Katharine was 24. A graduate of Oberlin College, she had just started teaching English and Latin in Dayton's principal high school.

Wilbur and Orville were "as inseparable as twins," their father recalled. Wilbur had been a promising student in high school and his father had hoped to send him to Yale. But illness kept him at home, where for several years he read studiously in his father's library and looked after his dying mother while the bishop traveled on church business.

Wilbur and Orville Wright

Wilbur (left) and Orville Wright on the back porch of the Hawthorn Street house, Dayton, Ohio, in June 1909.
(Wright State University Library)

"I have been interested in the problem of mechanical and human flight ever since as a boy I constructed a number of bats of various sizes after the style of Cayley's and Pénaud's machines," began the letter to the secretary of the Smithsonian Institution in Washington, D.C.

"I am about to begin a systematic study of the subject in preparation for practical work to which I expect to devote what time I can spare from my regular business. I wish to obtain such papers as the

1

of foolhardiness. Their earthbound fellow citizens cheered their achievements and made them celebrities, like movie stars and sports heroes. The hero aviators made aviation exciting, then familiar, and finally accepted.

Then their day passed. With the coming of World War II, the public's attention turned to more urgent matters. Aviation emerged from the war a bigger business than ever, and in business teamwork and anonymity are prized. The new challenge was space, and space exploration required the concentrated resources of the state, not clever mechanics and daredevil pilots.

Today, in the age of astronauts, space shuttles, and interplanetary space probes, the hero aviators look almost quaint in their windbreakers, riding breeches, leather helmets, and goggles. We marvel that they risked their lives in their fragile machines to accomplish what we now do so casually. But as they recede into history, these pioneers take on the stature of folk heroes, the Daniel Boones and Davy Crocketts of our century, men and women who embodied virtues that all Americans like to think are theirs—skill, daring, determination, optimism—and who together changed the world.

Introduction

airplane"—tractor because the engine pulled rather than pushed the plane forward. This design was safer for the pilot since, in the event of a crash, he would be behind and above the engine rather than beneath it.

World War I provided enormous stimulus to the development of airplanes. The fragile, mothlike crafts that provided observation for ground armies during the first months of the war were quickly superseded by fighting aircraft of many kinds—from small, speedy pursuit planes to large, multiengine bombers. Although few U.S.-built aircraft saw action in the war, the American Liberty engine was used by all Allied air forces.

For a short time after the war, aviation progressed slowly because of the large number of wartime planes that glutted the civilian market. But in laboratories and factories around the world, aeronautics was being transformed from the trial-and-error experimentation of inventive mechanics to a science embracing fields as diverse as metallurgy (the study of metals) and meteorology (the study of weather). First, the heavy water-cooled engines of World War I were replaced by light air-cooled engines of unprecedented reliability. Then, in the 1930s, wood-and-fabric biplanes (planes with two wings) gave way to all-metal monoplanes (planes with a single wing). The metal skin and monoplane design put an end to drag-causing struts, wires, and fixed landing gear. Strengthened airframes permitted greater fuel capacity and thus longer range. Finally, new radio and navigation equipment freed pilots from dependence on familiar landmarks. Commercial and military aircraft could now span continents and oceans.

One last obstacle remained to the realization of the full potential of piloted aircraft. With the development of the jet engine during World War II, air speeds increased until planes came alarmingly close to hitting the dreaded "sound barrier"—an imagined invisible wall of shock waves that a plane would encounter at the speed of sound. In some ways, fear of the sound barrier was like the fear once felt by early mariners sailing into unknown seas. The breaking of the sound barrier in 1947 banished this fear and opened a new era of supersonic flight.

All of this incredible technical progress was the work of legions of inventors, designers, mechanics, engineers, scientists, manufacturers, and capitalists—most of them nameless to the general public. The names we remember from aviation's pioneering years are those of the hero aviators. These men and women were young, adventurous, intoxicated by the thrill of flight, brave to the point

Wilbur and Orville Wright

Orville, less interested in studying, left high school after his junior year. A born tinkerer, he built a printing press out of scrap and established himself as a printer. Wilbur joined him in publishing a neighborhood newspaper for a time.

In 1893, responding to the craze for bicycling that was sweeping the country, the brothers opened a bicycle shop. In rented quarters at 1127 West Third Street, they created a machine shop, where they repaired, built and sold bicycles while a friend ran their small printing business.

But Wilbur was dissatisfied. Conscious of his intellectual powers, he felt he was growing older without accomplishing anything noteworthy. He wanted an activity that would challenge his capacities and perhaps lead on to fame and fortune. As children, he and Orville had been fascinated by a toy helicopter designed by a Frenchman, Alphonse Pénaud. During the 1890s, aeronautical experiments in Europe and America were receiving wide publicity. The challenge Wilbur resolved to confront was the problem of human flight.

From ancient times, people had dreamed of flying. They had observed fish swimming in water, birds flying in air. The analogy between the two media—water and air—was clear, the great difference being that air was so much less dense than water. In the 19th century, the development of the submarine reinforced the idea that if humans could navigate through water they should also be able to navigate through air. The invention of the balloon in the 18th century led eventually to the development of airships—blimps and dirigibles—moved by engine-driven propellers built on the same principle as the marine propellers that drove steamships. But these lighter-than-air craft, slow and cumbersome, did not satisfy people's desire to fly with the speed and freedom of birds.

Bird flight was always the model for aeronautical experimenters. When scientists discovered that the muscles used by a bird in flapping flight constituted a third or more of its body weight, many students of aeronautics (but certainly not all) realized that humans would never fly by muscle power. But birds also soared and glided without flapping their wings. Ornithologists observed that bird wings were not flat but arched or "cambered"—that is, they had a convex curve from front to back. Without understanding why cambered wings were necessary for flight, experimenters believed that it should be possible to soar and glide on human-made wings constructed on the same design. When such wings

3

were combined with a steam or gasoline engine driving a propeller, the result would be powered flight in a heavier-than-air craft.

In the 1890s the construction of a flying machine seized the imaginations of many mechanics and inventors—and a good number of crackpots, too. Every day, it seemed, some village inventor, strapped into a homemade contraption shaped like a bat, a bird, or even a fish, was jumping off a barn or cliff, only to fall to earth in a heap of sticks and fabric.

But there were also serious investigators at work on the problem of flight. In Germany, Otto Lilienthal completed nearly 2,000 short flights in bird-shaped gliders between 1891 and his death in a glider crash in 1896. His vehicles were hang gliders in which he stood upright between the wings, controlling the craft (insofar as he could) by shifting his weight and thereby the glider's center of gravity.

Also in 1896, on the shore of Lake Michigan near Chicago, engineer Octave Chanute and his young associates tested a variety of glider types, the most successful of which were modeled after Lilienthal's. And in that same year, at Quantico, Virginia, near Washington, D.C., Samuel Pierpont Langley, secretary of the Smithsonian Institution, flew a steam-powered model aircraft with a 14-foot wingspan for 90 seconds.

The well-publicized death of Otto Lilienthal reawakened in Wilbur and Orville Wright their childhood interest in flying. Over the next three years that interest absorbed Wilbur increasingly. Determined to learn all that was then known about aeronautics, he wrote to the Smithsonian Institution for help on May 30, 1899. He received in reply a package of four articles reprinted from the *Smithsonian Annual Report* and a list of books for further reading.

Wilbur soon realized that the problems of wing design and power for an aircraft had already been largely solved. The great remaining problem, which no one else seemed to appreciate, was that of controlling an aircraft once it was in the air. Such a craft would be free to rotate around three axes—a horizontal axis running from wing tip to wing tip (rotation around this axis is called pitch), another horizontal axis running from the nose of the craft to its tail (rotation around which is called roll), and a vertical axis running through the center of the craft (rotation around this axis is called yaw).

Yaw and pitch might be controlled (with great difficulty, as it turned out) by horizontal and vertical rudders like those on a submarine. The true problem was roll. In a glider, the pilot controlled roll by shifting his weight. But this was a hazardous expedient, possible only on a small craft. All other students of aeronautics wanted to build a craft that would be stable—that would resist roll or would right itself automatically if a gust of wind caused it to roll—without the pilot's intervention. Such a craft would fly a level course. When its vertical rudder was activated, it would make a wide, flat turn without rolling.

Wilbur believed that the pilot must be able to control roll as well as pitch and yaw. Indeed, the pilot should be able to induce roll in making a turn. Wilbur observed that birds rolled or banked when they turned, raising one wing and lowering the other. Similarly, bicycle riders leaned into their turns. Controlling and using roll was essential for true flying.

Wilbur and Orville Wright would eventually make many contributions to the design of aircraft, affecting wings, rudders, propellers, and engines. But their first and crucial contribution was their technique of "wing warping," which enabled them not only to correct for roll while in straight flight but also induce roll to make a banking turn. In wing warping, the pilot actually twisted the flexible wings of his craft so that the outer edges of one pair of wings were raised while those of the opposite pair were simultaneously lowered. When early Wright airplanes banked in making turns, observers knew they were seeing true flying machines.

In July 1899, only weeks after receiving the package of articles from the Smithsonian, Wilbur was ready to test his ideas about controlling an aircraft in flight. He built a kite consisting of two wings, each five feet long and 13 inches wide, firmly joined by vertical struts and crossed wires. A horizontal rudder, or elevator, was fixed midway between them at the rear of the kite. Strings leading from the tops and bottoms of the two outboard struts to sticks held in each hand enabled Wilbur to manipulate the kite. At his command, the kite dove, climbed, and rolled left and right.

Excitedly, the brothers set to work to build a passenger-carrying glider out of wood and fabric. Their machine, like the kite, was a biplane. Its shallow-cambered wings were 17 feet five inches long and five feet wide, providing a total wing area of 165 square feet. The horizontal rudder, or elevator, was now placed in front of the wings. There was no vertical rudder. The pilot would lie in a cutout on the lower wing, able to raise or lower the elevator with his hands while at the same time using his feet to operate cables that caused the wings to twist. The glider weighed just 50 pounds.

But where would they fly this machine? The brothers calculated that they would need steady headwinds of 15 miles an hour to loft their glider. They would also need good weather, a soft place to land, and seclusion from inquisitive strangers. With information provided by the U.S. Weather Bureau, they found an ideal place—the little settlement of Kitty Hawk on a remote beach in North Carolina.

In October 1900 Wilbur and Orville assembled their glider on the dunes near Kitty Hawk. At first they flew it unmanned, like a kite. Then Wilbur made a number of glides, eventually achieving flights of 300 to 400 feet lasting 15 seconds. But the glider was not lifting as readily as they had calculated, and there were problems with the controls. They must apply the information they had obtained that October, all carefully recorded, in building a new glider.

The brothers were back at Kitty Hawk in July 1901 with a new glider. The wings, now deeply cambered, were 22 feet long and seven feet wide, promising much greater lift. But in fact, the new machine was less satisfactory than the old. Even after they remodeled the elevator and wings, the craft did not achieve the lift they expected, and wing warping did not give them the lateral control— balance and turning—they hoped for. Gloomily, they returned to Dayton in August.

Thus far the Wrights had designed their gliders using information from other experimenters. It was clear now that much of that information was wrong. They would have to test and measure everything themselves. That fall they built a wind tunnel in their bicycle shop. A wooden box six feet long and 16 inches square, it had a glass window on its top. A fan at one end drove a steady wind at 27 miles per hour through the tunnel. On a balance in the center of the tunnel, which they could view through the glass window, they tested the efficiency of some 150 different airfoils—the curved ribs that gave the glider's wings their shape—at all possible angles. They also tested the shape of wing tips and the ideal distance between two wings. At last they had data they could rely on.

In September 1902 they were back at Kitty Hawk with a new glider. The wings now spanned 32 feet but were only five feet wide. More important, they were curved in the way that had proved most efficient in wind-tunnel tests—a camber of 1/20 (an arch with a ratio of one inch in height for each 20 inches of length) with its peak a quarter of the way back from the wing's leading edge. The horizontal rudder, or elevator, still protruded far ahead of the wings. Now there was a double, fixed vertical rudder at the tail.

This machine was beginning to look like later airplanes rather than like a box kite.

The 1902 glider exceeded all expectations, particularly after the brothers substituted a single, movable vertical rudder for the fixed double rudder with which they had started. Flights exceeding 500 feet became common. On October 23, Wilbur piloted the craft 622.5 feet in 26 seconds, a new record for flight distance and duration. For the first time, Orville went aloft and, with his brother shouting instructions from the ground, taught himself to fly. The next step was powered flight.

The 1903 machine assembled at Kitty Hawk weighted 675 pounds. It was very similar to the 1902 machine but larger and stronger—and, unlike the 1902 version, it was powered. A 12-horsepower gasoline engine built in the bicycle shop drove two pusher propellers mounted on the trailing edges of the wings and turning in opposite directions. The machine would take off from a 60-foot rail on which it rode on bicycle-wheel hubs.

The craft was ready on December 14. The brothers tossed a coin. Wilbur won and took his position on the lower wing. The plane raced down the rail, mounted steeply into the air, stalled, and fell to earth. Repairs took two days.

On December 17 it was Orville's turn. At 10:35 that morning, with Wilbur running alongside holding up one wing, the plane clattered down the launching rail into a 21-mile-per-hour headwind, rose unsteadily into the air, and traveled 120 feet before striking the sand. The first powered flight in history had lasted 12 seconds.

There were several more flights that morning, each longer than the preceding one. Wilbur and Orville took turns as pilot. About noon, Wilbur covered 852 feet in 59 seconds. Then, while the plane was being readied for another flight, a gust of wind overturned it, and the plane was wrecked. In the past they had abandoned their gliders on the beach, but this time Wilbur and Orville collected the pieces of the world's first airplane for return to Dayton. That afternoon Orville telegraphed their father:

Success. Four flights Thursday morning. All against twenty-one mile wind. Started from level with engine power alone. Average speed through air thirty-one miles. Longest 57 [actually 59] seconds. Inform press. Home Christmas.

With a powered aircraft, the Wrights no longer needed the winds of Kitty Hawk. The scene of their work now shifted to

The first powered flight in history, near Kitty Hawk, North Carolina, 10:35 A.M., December 17, 1903. Orville Wright is the pilot, Wilbur runs alongside.
(Wright State University Library)

Huffman Prairie, a 100-acre cow pasture eight miles east of Dayton, which they could reach by city and interurban trolley. There, in 1904 and 1905, they improved their machines and perfected their skill at flying. Their 1904 "Flyer," almost a replica of the 1903 craft, had difficulty getting up to air speed on the long rail that was still used for takeoffs. Most flights were short hops of a hundred feet or so that frequently ended in crashes. Not until September did Orville manage to stay aloft more than a minute and a half, making one complete circuit of the pasture. Their 1905 plane, significantly modified after early disappointments, was a vast improvement. On October 5, Wilbur circled the pasture 30 times, traveling almost 25 miles in 40 minutes.

The first report of the Wrights' 59-second flight at Kitty Hawk was rejected by the Dayton *Journal* as not newsworthy; a few newspapers around the country printed a garbled account of the event. In January 1904 the brothers provided an accurate account, which circulated in the United States and Europe. But reporters who visited Huffman Prairie in 1904 and 1905 were not impressed by what they saw. Local people, however, riding by on the interurban trolley or hanging on the pasture fence, were astonished, and rumors of the Wrights' activities spread swiftly.

The Wrights did not want publicity before they had patented and sold their invention. After their successful flights of 1905, they ceased flying altogether. They refused to exhibit their machine or even to show photographs of it. And they refused to participate in public demonstrations or competitions that would have earned them substantial sums. Their secrecy was not motivated by greed; what they wanted was recognition.

For two years, 1906 and 1907, the Wrights were out of the public eye. Their efforts to sell their invention to the governments of the United States, Great Britain, France, and Germany were rebuffed. The problem was that the Wrights refused to demonstrate their airplane before they had a purchase contract. There was no risk to the purchaser; no money would change hands if the plane did not meet the purchaser's specifications. But no government official would risk making a fool of himself by buying a flying machine before he had seen it fly.

The suspicion grew that the Wrights were fakes, like so many other self-proclaimed inventors of flying machines. After all, if they could fly, why didn't they prove it? But for the sons of Bishop Wright, it was a question of their integrity. They expected to be taken at their word. Until their terms were met, they would wait, confident that they were years ahead of other experimenters.

In Europe and America, experimenters were busy with gliders and powered machines inspired by reports of the Wrights' achievements and by incomplete descriptions of the Wrights' airplane. In France, the Brazilian airship pioneer Alberto Santos-Dumont created a sensation in November 1906 when he flew his biplane more than 700 feet. And Henri Farman was acclaimed in January 1908 for flying a circular course of one mile. In the United States in July 1908, Glenn Curtiss won the first *Scientific American* trophy for flying his *June Bug* more than a mile in a straight line.

The Wrights made no public comments. They did not consider any of these craft to be practical flying machines comparable to their own. But the questioning became ever more insistent: Where are the Wrights? As one newspaper asked, are they "fliers or liars?"

In 1908, both the U.S. Army and a group of French investors met the Wrights' terms: a signed contract *before* a demonstration flight. The new Wright plane had improved controls as well as upright seats for the pilot and a passenger. It still took off from a rail rather than on wheels. On August 8, 1908, Wilbur took to the

Orville Wright demonstrating the Wright Flyer at Fort Myer, Virginia, September 1908.
(Wright State University Library)

air near Le Mans, France, in his first public flight since 1905. For a week, before growing crowds, he circled the Hunaudières race-track, banking steeply into turns, tracing tight figure eights. Flying like this had never been seen before. The crowds were stunned, the newspapers ecstatic.

On September 3, at Fort Myer, Virginia, Orville began his demonstration flights for the U.S. Army. Day by day, the crowds grew larger, the flights longer. On September 12 he set an endurance record of more than an hour and a quarter. Several times he carried a passenger, as his contract with the army required. On September 17, with an army officer beside him, Orville had completed two circles of the parade ground when one of his two propellers split. The plane dove into the ground. Orville was seriously injured; his passenger was killed.

After 1908 Wilbur and Orville Wright were international celebrities. In Europe and America, awestruck multitudes breathlessly watched their soaring flights. Honors were heaped upon them. Their achievement was at last universally recognized—although they knew that it would be only a short time before others caught up with and even surpassed them.

Wilbur and Orville Wright

A Wright Company was founded in 1909, with Wilbur as president and Orville as vice president. Headquarters were in New York, but the company's factory was in Dayton, and there Wilbur and Orville worked on the development of new Wright airplanes.

On May 30, 1912, Wilbur died of typhoid fever in Dayton. Orville became president of the company, but three years later he sold it, and thereafter he worked independently in his Dayton laboratory. He received patents for an automatic pilot and for a type of wing flap that proved useful on dive bombers in World War II. In 1920 President Woodrow Wilson appointed him to the National Advisory Committee for Aeronautics. But most of his time was spent in his laboratory tinkering with household gadgets.

Neither Wilbur nor Orville ever married. When their sister Katharine finally married in 1926, Orville felt betrayed. Brother and sister were not reconciled until just before Katharine's death in 1929. Orville died of a heart attack in Dayton on January 30, 1948.

The respective contributions of Wilbur and Orville Wright to the invention of the airplane were long obscured. Because he outlived his brother for many years, Orville alone received public attention and recognition as the inventor. Not until the publication of *The Papers of Wilbur and Orville Wright* (2 volumes, 1953) did it become clear that it was the older brother, Wilbur, who selected flight as his field of study, who recognized that lateral control was the crucial problem to be solved, and who, almost immediately, conceived its solution with the technique of wing warping. This achievement, entirely Wilbur's, was indispensable to the development of a practical airplane.

But the actual building of a machine that would fly—and learning to fly it—was another matter. And here Orville was an equal partner with his older brother. When it became clear that the aeronautical data they had received from earlier experimenters were incorrect, they had to reinvent the science of aeronautics from scratch. Wilbur and Orville together, for example, built the world's first wind tunnel and discovered, by careful observation and measurement, how to shape a wing capable of flight. Through years of dangerous practice, both brothers taught themselves how to fly.

The invention of the airplane was perhaps the most startling in the entire history of invention. Contemporaries received news of the airplane with disbelief. Even when they actually saw it fly, they could scarcely believe their eyes. Ordinary people considered the airplane a mere curiosity, an outlandish and useless contraption. Wiser people sensed at once that the airplane was the forerunner of a new age. Not only would it shorten distances between cities and countries, but it would transform the relations of peoples, in war and in peace, for better or for worse. The frontiers that separated nations would cease to exist. And indeed, when the French aviator Louis Blériot flew the English Channel in 1909, Britons realized with alarm that their island nation was no longer securely isolated from the continent of Europe. Many early aviation enthusiasts saw the airplane as a means of increasing friendship among nations; military planners, however, saw its less peaceful implications.

Wilbur Wright died at age 45, before World War I; Orville died at 77. Orville lived to see all the prophecies about the impact of the airplane on human life fulfilled. He lived to see the skies filled with fleets of bombers. But he also lived to see the world knit together more closely by networks of freight and passenger air routes. In the last year of his life he may have read that an American pilot had flown faster than the speed of sound.

On December 17, 1948, the 45th anniversary of its first successful flight at Kitty Hawk, the original Wright Flyer was ceremonially installed at the Smithsonian Institution in Washington, D.C. The plaque next to the strange-looking flying machine read: "The original Wright brothers aeroplane, the world's first power-driven, heavier-than-air machine in which man made free, controlled, and sustained flight, invented and built by Wilbur and Orville Wright, flown by them at Kitty Hawk, North Carolina, December 17, 1903. By original scientific research, the Wright brothers discovered the principles of human flight. As inventors, builders, and flyers, they further developed the aeroplane, taught man to fly, and opened the era of aviation."

Chronology

April 16, 1867	Wilbur Wright born in Millville, Indiana
August 19, 1871	Orville Wright born in Dayton, Ohio
1893	the brothers open a bicycle shop in Dayton
1899	Wilbur becomes interested in flight, writes to the Smithsonian

	Institution for help, conceives and tests wing warping as the solution to the problem of lateral control
1900	at Kitty Hawk, North Carolina, the brothers fly a passenger-glider
1901	the brothers build the first wind tunnel, accumulate new aeronautical data
1902	continue glider experiments at Kitty Hawk
1903	Orville, then Wilbur, make powered flights at Kitty Hawk
1904	continue flying experiments at Huffman Prairie, outside of Dayton
1905	cease public flying, begin search for buyers
1908	with buyers committed, Wilbur demonstrates flying machine at Le Mans, France, and Orville demonstrates it at Fort Myer, Virginia
1909	Wright Company incorporated with Wilbur as president, Orville as vice president
May 30, 1912	Wilbur dies at Dayton, Ohio
1915	Orville sells interest in Wright Company, thereafter lives privately in Dayton
January 30, 1948	Orville dies in Dayton, Ohio

Further Reading

Crouch, Tom D. *The Bishop's Boys: A Life of Wilbur and Orville Wright*. New York: W. W. Norton, 1989. The most recent of many Wright biographies, this is a thorough, fascinating, and fair account, equally strong on the men and their technology.

Crouch provides interesting insights into the family and the personalities of the inventors.

Howard, Fred. *Wilbur and Orville: A Biography of the Wright Brothers*. New York: Knopf, 1987. An excellent biography, judicious and well-rounded, by the aeronautics librarian at the Library of Congress. It is particularly strong on the Wrights' relations with their contemporaries.

Walsh, John E. *One Day at Kitty Hawk: The Untold Story of the Wright Brothers and the Airplane*. New York: Crowell, 1975. This young-adult book carries the Wright story only to 1909, emphasizing Wilbur's preeminent contribution.

Westcott, Lynanne, and Paul Degen. *Wind and Sand: The Story of the Wright Brothers at Kitty Hawk*. New York: Abrams, 1983. The great feature of this book is 102 black-and-white photographs, taken from 1900 through 1911, of the Wrights' experiments with gliders and their first airplanes.

Glenn H. Curtiss

Glenn Curtiss at the controls of the June Bug, *1908.*
(Glenn H. Curtiss Museum of Local History, Hammondsport, N.Y.)

*F*or a few years early in this century, the aviation capital of the United States was the village of Hammondsport on Keuka Lake in the winegrowing region of upstate New York. The fame of the little town was due entirely to a local boy, Glenn Hammond Curtiss, who was born there on May 21, 1878. Glenn finished the eighth grade at the Hammondsport Union Free School in 1892 and then worked at a variety of jobs—for Eastman Kodak and Western Union in Rochester, and then as a harness salesman, bicycle repairman, and photographer back in Hammondsport.

The young Glenn Curtiss was lean and muscular, of medium height, with dark hair and steady blue eyes. A thick mustache, a reserved and taciturn manner, and a perpetual thoughtful frown made him seem older than he was. Never a scholar, Curtiss was a born mechanic, businessman, and athlete. At 22 he operated a successful business manufacturing and selling bicycles. But he was more interested in racing bicycles than in selling them. Starting in his teens with other Hammondsport boys, Curtiss traveled the county fair racing circuit, usually winning the prize money.

He did not like to lose. Legend has it that after a particularly humiliating loss, he installed a mail-order gasoline engine on one of his bicycles; this launched him on a new and even more notable career as a motorcycle racer. Soon he was building his own engines and motorcycles in a shop behind his house. Business expanded, along with his fame as a motorcycle racer and record setter. In Florida in 1907 he drove a motorcycle powered by a huge eight-cylinder Curtiss engine at a record speed of 136.3 miles per hour. Newspapers hailed Glenn Curtiss as "the fastest man in the world."

The fame of Curtiss's motorcycle engines reached as far as California. From San Francisco in 1904 Curtiss received an order from "Captain" Tom Baldwin—a former circus performer who now specialized in building and exhibiting balloons—for a light, dependable engine capable of powering a dirigible. Over the next few years, Curtiss built a number of successful engines for Baldwin's dirigibles. When Baldwin's factory was destroyed in the San Francisco earthquake of 1906, he moved his business to Hammondsport to be near his engine-maker, whom he considered the key to his success. In 1908, Baldwin and Curtiss built and flew a dirigible that was bought by the U.S. Army one month before Orville Wright won an army contract for a heavier-than-air flying machine.

For a long time Curtiss thought that aviation enthusiasts were cranks, though he was happy to sell them his engines. Flying Baldwin's slow-moving gas bags did not thrill him as much as riding a good motorcycle. But as perhaps the country's leading expert on lightweight but powerful motors, Curtiss was drawn inevitably into the aborning science of aviation. In 1906 he accompanied Captain Baldwin to a dirigible show in Dayton, Ohio. There the two met the Wright brothers, and the four men discussed aeronautical problems. The Wrights—who had ceased public flying of their aircraft the previous year—showed photos of their machine in flight over Huffman Prairie but would not permit their visitors to see the machine itself. Curtiss's proposal to provide engines for the Wright brothers was declined.

That same year, Curtiss and Baldwin attended a show in New York sponsored by the Aero Club of America, a group of wealthy aeronautical buffs. Baldwin displayed a dirigible and Curtiss exhibited his motors. At the show Curtiss met Alexander Graham Bell, the inventor of the telephone. Then 60 years old, Bell was enthusiastic about artificial flight, which he believed would be accomplished with powered kites. He ordered an engine from Curtiss, and Curtiss personally delivered it to Bell's summer home in Nova Scotia, where the great inventor was building a huge passenger-carrying kite consisting of thousands of silk-covered tetrahedral cells arranged in layers. Alas, the kite was wrecked on a test flight before the engine could be installed.

Bell had recruited three young men, all graduate engineers, to assist him in his work. They, Bell, and Curtiss formed the Aerial Experiment Association (AEA) with funds supplied by Mrs. Bell. Bell hoped his associates would continue his work with kites, but the four young men were more interested in airplanes like those of the Wright brothers and European experimenters—although none of them had actually seen one. They determined that the site of their work should be Hammondsport, and in January 1908 they all moved there—Dr. and Mrs. Bell and the four younger members of the AEA. In fact, they all moved into Curtiss's commodious old house on the outskirts of town, located right in front of his ever-expanding motorcycle and engine factory and not far from Baldwin's dirigible works. Thus did the little village of Hammondsport become a center of aeronautics.

Dr. and Mrs. Bell soon returned to their home in Washington, while the young men of the AEA set to work. First they experimented with small biplane gliders, redesigning wings and tails as experience directed. Between mid-January and early March they built their first powered flying machine. A biplane, it closely resembled the Wrights' flying machine, pictures of which Curtiss had seen in Dayton. Its tapered wings, arched rather than horizontal, spanned 43 feet. Bamboo poles supported the horizontal elevator seven feet in front of the wings and a fixed tail and square rudder ten feet behind. An eight-cylinder Curtiss engine behind the pilot drove a steel pusher propeller. The machine was equipped with runners to take off and land on the ice of Keuka Lake. Because the spruce frames of its wings were covered with red silk, the machine was called *Red Wing*.

On March 12, 1908, *Red Wing*, whose pilot had been chosen by lot, sped 200 feet across the ice of Keuka Lake, rose perhaps 10 feet into the air, then rolled to the right, a wing striking the ice and spinning the craft around. The machine had flown nearly 320 feet. On March 17 *Red Wing* flew again, but almost immediately it rolled to the left and crashed. In neither mishap was the pilot hurt, but in the second the machine was demolished.

Writing from Washington, Bell stressed the importance of lateral control to prevent the rolling that had been fatal to *Red Wing*. The Wrights had achieved this by "wing warping," but their method was protected by patent, and in any case the members of the AEA considered a flexible wing to be structurally unsound. Bell suggested hingeing to the wing tips triangular flaps wired to a harness worn by the pilot. If the craft rolled to the left, the pilot would lean to the right, causing the tips of the left wings to rise and those of the right wings to depress, thereby righting the machine.

These triangular wing tips, later called ailerons, were installed on the AEA's second machine. This craft, powered by the eight-cylinder engine salvaged from *Red Wing*, was slightly smaller than its predecessor and was equipped with wheels rather than runners. Its propeller was made of laminated spruce. Because silk was expensive, the wings were covered with white cotton fabric. When the cotton cloth proved too porous to provide lift, a coat of varnish solved the problem. The color of the cotton fabric determined the name of the second AEA machine: *White Wing*.

For their next experiments, the owner of Stony Book Farm, two miles outside of Hammondsport, offered the men of the AEA the use of a racetrack for trotters on his property, where the young Curtiss had once raced bicycles. On May 18 and 19, 1908, *White Wing* made three short flights there, the longest 93 yards. On May 21, Curtiss's thirtieth birthday, it was his turn to fly—his first time ever at the controls of a heavier-than-air machine. He covered 339 yards (1,017 feet) in two "jumps," *White Wing*'s wheels briefly touching the ground after the first 205 yards. The flight lasted only 19 seconds, but the pilot had time to steer left and right, demonstrating that the craft was truly under his control. Curtiss was elated. This was a totally new experience. A skeptic no longer, he was now an aviator.

Curtiss directed construction of the AEA's third machine. He made a number of modifications in the design of *White Wing*, but the most significant was his further development of the hinged wing tips or ailerons suggested by Dr. Bell and first employed on *White Wing* to achieve lateral stability.

On the Wright machine, lateral stability was achieved by wing warping. Wing warping, in fact, had two uses. First, it enabled the pilot to correct for roll. Second, it enabled the pilot to *induce* roll when, also employing the rudder, he made a banking turn. But when used in straight flight merely to correct for roll, wing warping had a turning effect, since it caused a differential in the "drag" on opposite wings. This turning effect had to be countered by using the rudder. In the Wright machine, therefore, the wing-warping and rudder controls were necessarily connected.

On his new machine, Curtiss enlarged the ailerons but also altered their angle of incidence, or slope. Instead of placing them at the same angle as the wings to which they were attached, he fixed them at a neutral angle—that is, parallel to the ground. The result was that when one aileron was raised and the other lowered, the angles of incidence remained the same, producing no differential in drag and therefore no turning effect. Thus Curtiss could control for roll using his ailerons alone without his rudder. In making a banking turn, of course, he would use the ailerons and rudder together. But ailerons and rudder were not connected. This rather technical point, difficult for a nonaviator to appreciate, was at the heart of Curtiss's case in a long and bitter patent dispute with the Wright brothers.

Another change in the new machine was its color. To make the machine easy to photograph, yellow paint was added to the varnish used to coat the cotton wing fabric. The new machine was called *June Bug*.

On June 21, 1908, a month after his first flight in *White Wing*, Curtiss made three short flights in *June Bug*, the longest 725 yards at an altitude of 40 feet. Two days later he made two more flights, the longer one covering 1,140 yards. This was more than the one kilometer (3,279 feet) that the Aero Club of America had fixed as the requirement for the award of the first *Scientific American* trophy. Curtiss promptly informed the Aero Club that he was ready to compete officially for the trophy, exercising his right to select the location of the flight. He chose Hammondsport.

On July 4, 1908, almost the entire population of Hammondsport gathered at Stony Book Farm to witness the much-anticipated flight. An official delegation from the Aero Club and a crowd of reporters and photographers came all the way from New York City for the event. Unfortunately, the day was windy and rainy, and *June Bug* remained in its protective tent. Late in the afternoon, however, the weather began to clear. At six o'clock *June Bug* was wheeled from its tent to the starting line on the racetrack. A red flag on a post a kilometer away across vineyards and potato fields marked the finish line. By seven o'clock, after careful preparation,

The June Bug, *piloted by Curtiss, winning the* Scientific American *trophy
on July 4, 1908, at Hammondsport.*
(Glenn H. Curtiss Museum of Local History, Hammondsport, N.Y.)

Curtiss was ready. But his first attempt had to be aborted because the machine's tail had been incorrectly mounted. The machine was pulled back to the starting line, and at 7:30 Curtiss took off again.

"The machine," recalled one witness, "which was 20 feet or more above our heads, seemed to slowly descend until it was not more than 10 or 15 feet high, but it did not go lower. Directly over the stake it steered, rising higher as it went, and away it soared over the fences, turning to the left and settling gently down in a pasture over a mile away from where it left the race course."

(It must be remembered that three years before this, the Wright brothers were routinely making flights as long as 25 miles. But the Wrights avoided publicity and after 1905 refused to exhibit their machine.)

Winning the *Scientific American* trophy made Glenn Curtiss famous. Later that summer, their sensational demonstration flights at Le Mans, France, and Fort Myer, Virginia, made Wilbur and Orville Wright even more famous.

Aviation was all the rage, but there were few customers for airplanes. The government bought some for experimental purposes, and a handful of wealthy sportsmen expressed interest in the dangerous novelty. Every flying machine was handmade, and the purchase price included flight instruction as well. The only money to be made from aviation was in exhibition flying or in competing for prizes offered by newspapers, organizations, or others interested in promoting the new technology or simply in garnering publicity for themselves. The Wright brothers dismissed this sort of activity with contempt as "mountebank flying." But Curtiss was a born competitor with a lust for speed and an irresistible passion for flying. Furthermore, the money to be made by "prize chasing and exhibition work" was not inconsiderable.

Early in 1909, the Aeronautical Society of New York ordered a flying machine from Curtiss. For its $5,000, the society was to get not only the airplane but flying lessons for two of its members and a public demonstration by Curtiss, at which the society hoped to earn back its investment. Curtiss designed a small, compact biplane with straight, untapered wings rather than the arched and tapered wings of *June Bug*. He moved the ailerons from the wing tips to the struts midway between the two wings. And he powered the machine with a four-cylinder water-cooled engine.

On June 26, 1909, 5,000 New Yorkers paid $1 each to get into Morris Park racetrack in the Bronx to see an aerial show that included balloons, kites, and gliders. The featured attraction was Curtiss's new *Gold Bug*, the first airplane that New Yorkers had seen. After a few short straight flights, Curtiss circled the track, a feat of controlled flight that drove the crowd wild.

Borrowing the successful *Gold Bug* from the Aeronautical Society, Curtiss next went to Hempstead Plains near Mineola, Long Island, to take up the offer of the Aero Club of America of the second *Scientific American* trophy to the first person to fly 25 kilometers (15.5 miles) around a triangular one-and-a-third-mile course. On July 17, Curtiss circled the course 19 times in some 52 minutes, covering 24.7 miles and winning the coveted trophy for the second year in a row.

His next stop was France. The Aéro Club de France had scheduled an international flying meet at Rheims for August 22–29 in which all the famous aviators of Europe would participate. The most notable among them was the Frenchman Louis Blériot, who on July 25, 1909, became the first person to fly across the English Channel—winning, in the process, $5,000 offered by the British newspaper publisher Lord Northcliffe, plus $2,500 put up by a French wine company. In addition to the other prizes offered at

Rheims, the American newspaper publisher James Gordon Bennett announced a silver trophy and $5,000 in cash for the pilot who achieved the greatest speed over a closed course.

Curtiss determined to win the Bennett trophy. He had a new plane, small like the *Gold Bug* but powered by an advanced eight-cylinder engine. Some of the other pilots brought more than one airplane and teams of mechanics to Rheims; Curtiss, the only American to compete, arrived with a single machine and one mechanic. Seven events were scheduled for airplanes during the week, with the Bennett trophy race next to last. Unwilling to risk his single plane on lesser events, Curtiss bided his time while other aviators set new records for speed, altitude, distance, and endurance.

The race for the Bennett trophy was held on Saturday, August 28. The prescribed distance, 20 kilometers (12.4 miles), meant two circuits of a rectangular 10-kilometer course whose four corners were marked by red and white pylons. Five aviators qualified for the race, three of them French; Blériot was the heavy favorite. They were to fly singly, at any time during the day they chose. At 10 A.M., before 50,000 spectators, Curtiss took off in his little biplane. He circled for altitude, then like an experienced bicycle racer dived across the starting line at maximum speed. On the straightaways he climbed to 50 feet, shaved the pylons in steep banking turns, then dove again to regain speed. He finished the course in 15 minutes, 50 seconds, for an average speed of 46.5 miles per hour.

Blériot did not fly until late afternoon. His first circuit in his mothlike monoplane was faster than Curtiss's, but a wide turn on his second circuit cost him the race. He finished six seconds behind Curtiss. Newspapers hailed Curtiss as "the world's champion aviator." The celebration spread from Rheims to Hammondsport.

On to Italy, where in September the Royal Aero Club was sponsoring another international air meet at Brescia. The celebrity of the hour, Curtiss was the idol of exuberant Italian crowds. He had no difficulty winning a speed contest over a 50-kilometer course. When he finally sailed from Cherbourg for New York on September 15, Curtiss carried $15,000 in prize money.

Back in New York, Curtiss was scheduled to fly in the Hudson–Fulton celebration marking the tricentennial of Henry Hudson's discovery of the Hudson River in 1609 and (a little belatedly) the centennial of Robert Fulton's steamboat trip up the Hudson in 1807. The celebration committee had also managed to coax Wilbur Wright to participate—Wright was paid $15,000, Curtiss

$5,000—in what the public interpreted as a competition between the world's two greatest aviators.

The aviators were based on Governors Island in New York Harbor. Curtiss did not have the plane he had used at Rheims. Instead, he had to use a new and untested plane powered by a four-cylinder engine. Throughout his stay, from September 25 to October 3, the weather was foul. He made two feeble flights, the longest barely half a mile long. The event truly belonged to Wilbur Wright. On September 29 Wright made a dramatic circle of the Statue of Liberty, in the process passing over the outbound liner *Lusitania*, whose decks were jammed with passengers. Then on October 4 Wright made a sensational 20-mile flight from Governors Island up the Hudson River, which was crowded with naval vessels, to Grant's Tomb on Manhattan's Riverside Drive and back again, a flight cheered by millions of New Yorkers.

Dramatic aerial performances at the St. Louis Centennial celebration in October 1909 and at an international air meet in Los Angeles in January 1910 did not erase Curtiss's chagrin at his failure in New York. To do that, he determined to make a flight from Albany to New York City for which the New York *World* had offered a prize of $10,000. The flight, over a distance of 152 miles, had to be made within a 24-hour period, and no more than two landings would be permitted en route. Back at Hammondsport, Curtiss built a new plane, similar to his Rheims racer but larger, and powered by an improved eight-cylinder engine. Because he would be flying over water, he contrived flotation gear that would keep the plane afloat in case of a river landing.

At 7:02 A.M. on May 29, 1910, in perfect weather, Curtiss took off from Van Rensselaer Island at the south edge of Albany, climbed to 700 feet, then headed south down the Hudson. At 8:26 he landed at a preselected meadow three miles south of Poughkeepsie, refueled, and was airborne again in an hour. Near Storm King Mountain in the Hudson Highlands, he was severely buffeted by winds. Descending to an altitude of 40 feet, he flew on. As the towers of Manhattan came into view, he discovered that his oil was critically low. At 10:25 he made an emergency landing on a wide green lawn at the northern end of Manhattan Island.

Because he had landed within the New York City limits, Curtiss had satisfied the requirements for the prize offered by the *World*. But he was determined to complete his flight and land at Governors Island. Repaired and refueled, his plane took off again at 11:42 and continued down the Hudson. The west side of Manhattan was crowded with spectators cheering him on. Leaving Manhattan behind, he circled the Statue of Liberty, then glided to a safe landing on Governors Island at noon. He had been in the air a total of two hours and 51 minutes and had flown at an average speed of 52 miles per hour.

For this feat, Curtiss received not only the *World*'s $10,000 prize but the *Scientific American* trophy for the third consecutive year. He had also erased the shame of his failure at the Hudson–Fulton celebration the year before. But most important, he had demonstrated the feasibility of dependable intercity flight.

As soon as Curtiss began to make money from manufacturing and flying airplanes—beginning with his sale of a machine to the Aero Club of New York in 1909—the Wright brothers sued, alleging infringement of their patents. The heart of their case was that lateral stability in an airplane was impossible without the altering of the angles of the wing, and that their patented technique of wing warping (used in conjunction with the rudder) covered any method that achieved the same effect. Curtiss's defense was that the wings on his machine were not flexible but rigid; that he achieved lateral stability by the use of ailerons, which were not part of the wing surface at all—in fact, they were soon transferred from the wing tips to the struts; and that the ailerons achieved lateral stability without simultaneous use of the rudder.

The suit made the Wrights extremely unpopular in aviation circles. They were accused of seeking to monopolize aviation, if not out of greed then out of desire for prestige. The suit certainly had the effect of impeding the progress of aviation in the United States. Curtiss stubbornly resisted, and the case dragged on with increasing bitterness on both sides until 1917, when, during World War I, all U.S. aviation patents were pooled to expedite the development of an America aviation industry. Ironically, in 1929, long after Wilbur Wright had died and Orville Wright and Glenn Curtiss had left the industry, the two great aviation companies founded by these pioneers merged to form the Curtiss-Wright Corporation.

Curtiss gave up exhibition flying in 1911, although he continued to employ an exhibition team of aerial daredevils, not only as a money-making enterprise but to advertise Curtiss-made airplanes and engines. He turned his attention to developing his business, particularly his business for the military. Curtiss was one of the first people to realize that the airplane could be more than a means of observation and communication for the armed services—that it could be an offensive weapon as well.

Glenn H. Curtiss

To enlarge the military market for his aircraft, Curtiss opened flying schools at Hammondsport and at North Island near San Diego, California, where he offered to train army and navy officers without charge. Curtiss was particularly interested in naval aviation, for he was convinced that bombs dropped from aircraft could destroy surface vessels. On January 18, 1911, a Curtiss exhibition pilot took off from the parade ground at the Presidio, an army post in San Francisco, landed his plane on a specially prepared platform aboard the battleship USS *Pennsylvania* anchored in the bay 13 miles offshore, and returned. The navy did not see much practical value in this unusual feat. What it wanted, it told Curtiss, was a plane that could land on the water next to a ship, be hoisted aboard like a boat, then returned to the water to fly again.

From his earliest aeronautical work at Hammondsport on the shore of Keuka Lake, Curtiss had believed that water afforded the best surface for aircraft to take off and land. In January 1909 he had attached pontoons to *June Bug* but was unable to get the plane to leave the surface of the lake. The problem of flying from water was not as simple as it appeared at first sight. Pontoons made the

A Curtiss airplane about to land on the stern of the USS Pennsylvania *in San Francicso Bay, February 17, 1911.*
(Glenn H. Curtiss Museum of Local History, Hammondsport, N.Y.)

25

plane heavier and more cumbersome. When the engine started, the pontoons tended to dig into the water. Furthermore, a strong suction held them to the surface.

Through tedious trial and error, Curtiss finally developed a single, shallow, flat-bottomed float that worked. On February 17, 1911, he flew his new hydroplane (or seaplane) from the water off North Island and landed beside the *Pennsylvania*, which was then at San Diego. He and his plane were hoisted aboard, then returned to the water, from which Curtiss took off again for North Island. The Navy was finally impressed. Shortly thereafter, Curtiss devised a retractable wheeled landing gear which, combined with the single float, converted his seaplane into an amphibian, a plane capable of taking off and landing on water or land.

Curtiss's next challenge was to build a flying boat. During 1912, first at North Island and then on Keuka Lake, he experimented with a variety of boat hulls. It was not difficult to attach wings to a boat hull, but no matter what shape was used, suction held the hull to the surface of the water. Finally, Curtiss conceived the idea of breaking the hold of the suction by attaching a wedge-shaped block to the bottom of the boat hull, its point facing forward and its straight rear forming a step. This wedge was screwed onto the hull he was then experimenting with. Almost miraculously, the boat lifted off the water and flew.

Curtiss sold several dozen flying boats to millionaires attracted to the fashionable new sport of "aero-yachting." More important were orders from foreign governments, which perceived the value of seaplanes and flying boats for patrolling coastal waters and vital sea lanes. When World War I began in the summer of 1914, foreign orders multiplied, and the Curtiss factory worked 24 hours a day. During the war, Curtiss flying boats, used as patrol-bombers, proved an effective weapon against German submarines.

The outbreak of war in Europe caused the U.S. government to take an urgent interest in its own military preparedness. Its scandalous neglect of aviation—in 1912, the United States spent less on aviation than France, Russia, Germany, and Great Britain, less even than Spain, Greece, and Bulgaria—was quickly remedied. Its first need was for a dual-control trainer in which pilot and student could fly together. Curtiss was ready with his new JN models, the famous "Jennies." This was his first tractor plane— that is, a plane in which the engine and propeller were placed in front of the pilot rather than behind him, pulling the plane forward rather than pushing it. It was a biplane with two open cockpits, one behind the other. Powered by an eight-cylinder, 100-horsepower engine, it was capable of flying 75 miles per hour. Almost all U.S. pilots trained during the war learned to fly in a Curtiss Army Jenny or its slightly modified navy version.

There was no room in Hammondsport for the wartime expansion of the Curtiss factory. In 1915, the business was moved to Buffalo, New York, where it continued to expand throughout the war. In 1916 Curtiss's various enterprises were reorganized as the Curtiss Aeroplane and Motor Corporation. Now a millionaire, Curtiss was a director and chairman of the board of the new corporation, but in reality, he conceded, he was only an employee. The firm had been organized by Wall Street financiers and it was run by industrial managers experienced in large-scale enterprises. The development of airplanes was no longer a trial-and-error affair where one "flew the bugs out," as Curtiss used to say; scientists and engineers designed and built the airplanes.

Curtiss was soon "exiled" from Buffalo to Garden City on Long Island, where he headed the Curtiss Engineering Corporation. He spent the war years there developing new types of aircraft. One of his projects was a four-engine flying boat designated the NC, but in 1918 the war ended before it could be put into service. This was a plane capable of realizing a dream that Curtiss had long cherished and almost made come true just before the war—a transatlantic flight. In May 1919, three NCs left Rockaway Naval Air Station on Long Island for Newfoundland, the Azores, Portugal and England. Only one—the NC-4—completed the trip, but its achievement marked the beginning of a new epoch in aviation.

After 1920, Curtiss had little further connection with aviation. "Aviation has passed me by," he explained. Moving to Florida, he made more millions in the Florida real estate boom of the 1920s. He maintained a summer home in Hammondsport, but the town's glory had departed. Gone were the dashing aviators, the bizarre dirigible works, the noisy Curtiss motorcycle and airplane factory. With the coming of Prohibition in 1919, even the local wineries closed down. Hammondsport became again the sleepy little village it had been when Curtiss was a boy.

In 1930, an aviation organization persuaded Curtiss to reenact his Albany-to-New York flight on the 20th anniversary of that event. This time, on May 30, 1930, Curtiss took off from Albany's new airport. He sat in the copilot's seat of a two-engine Curtiss Condor, a new eighteen-passenger airliner. Curtiss, who had not piloted a plane for many years, took the controls briefly over the

Hudson. At the end of the flight, he circled Governors Island, but it was the pilot who made the landing this time.

In July, Curtiss was stricken with appendicitis at his summer home in Hammondsport. He was taken to Buffalo and operated on at the Buffalo General Hospital. The operation was successful and he was recuperating normally, but on July 23, 1930, he died of a pulmonary embolism. He was 52 years old.

The Wright brothers must be credited with the invention of the airplane. They were also brave and skillful aviators. But the progress of American aviation from 1908 to 1918 was due in large measure to Glenn Curtiss. He was the first person after the Wrights to build and fly an airplane. The aileron, developed by Curtiss from an idea proposed by Alexander Graham Bell, was a crucial improvement over the Wrights' method of controlling a plane in flight by wing warping; in this respect, all modern airplanes descend from Curtiss's *June Bug* rather than from the Wright Flyers. Moreover, it was Curtiss who improved airplane engines from 40 horsepower to 400, who constantly developed new aircraft designs, who invented the seaplane, the amphibian, and the flying boat, who publicized the new technology by his dramatic exhibition flights. It was a life of ceaseless activity and remarkable achievement. "Right at the beginning," he said, "we learned an invaluable truth. We learned that so long as we were experimenting we never grew tired. Experimenting is never work—it is plain fun."

Chronology

May 21, 1878	born in Hammondsport, New York
1902	opens motorcycle shop in Hammondsport
1904	provides motorcycle engine for Thomas Baldwin's dirigible
1906	Curtiss and Baldwin meet the Wright brothers in Dayton
1907	drives motorcycle with unprecedented eight-cylinder engine 136.3 miles per hour at Ormond

	Beach, Florida; is called "the fastest man in the world"
1908	provides engine for the first dirigible purchased by the U.S. Army, builds and flies *June Bug*
1909	wins Bennett trophy at Rheims, France, but disappoints at New York's Hudson–Fulton celebration
1910	flies from Albany to New York with two stops, organizes the Curtiss Aeroplane Company
1911	flies first seaplane at North Island near San Diego, California
1912	flies first flying boat on Keuka Lake, New York
1915	Curtiss Aeroplane Company moves from Hammondsport to Buffalo, begins production of the Curtiss "Jenny"
1916	Curtiss Aeroplane and Motor Corporation organized
1919	Curtiss-built flying boat NC-4 crosses Atlantic from New York via Newfoundland and Azores to Lisbon
1920	leaves aviation industry
1930	reenacts Albany–New York flight
July 23, 1930	dies in Buffalo, New York

Further Reading

Roseberry, C. R. *Glenn Curtiss, Pioneer of Flight*. Garden City, N.Y.: Doubleday, 1972. A thorough, readable biography, with many black-and-white photos.

Scharff, Robert, and Walter S. Taylor. *Over Land and Sea: A Biography of Glenn Hammond Curtiss*. New York: D. McKay Co., 1968. A short, lively account of the inventor, aviation pioneer, and businessman.

Edward V. Rickenbacker

*Eddie Rickenbacker beside a Nieuport 28 fighter bearing
the hat-in-the-ring insignia of the 94th Aero Pursuit
Squadron, 1918.*
(Smithsonian Institution Photo No. A3853)

When the United States entered World War I in April 1917, the war
was already in its third year. On the western front, the armies of
Germany on one side and of France and Great Britain on the other
faced each other, deadlocked, across a no-man's-land between a
double line of trenches that ran across northern France from Swit-
zerland to the North Sea. Lives were squandered in the thousands
for territory measured in yards. Never before had there been a war
like this.

Above the carnage on the ground, another war was being fought
that was equally novel. This was the aerial war, fought by brave
young men in aircraft still made of wood and fabric. To civilians
back home, numbed by the spectacle of mass armies grappling in

the mud, the military aviators were romantic individualists, knights of the air dueling in single combat. Their exploits were celebrated like those of sports heroes. The aviators viewed themselves very much in the same way. They were a breed apart, a warrior elite, inheritors of an ideal of chivalry that had long since vanished from the battlefields.

When the war started, the airplane was barely 10 years old. At first, the few and fragile planes on both sides flew only unarmed observation missions. But the war speeded the development of better machines. By 1917, thousands of armed airplanes were engaged over the front. Observation was still a major activity. Two-seater observation and photoreconnaissance airplanes armed with machine guns could range far afield, unlike the observation balloons moored a mile or two behind the front. Slow-moving multiengine bombers, like the German Gotha, the British Handley-Page and the French Salmson, attacked rail yards and supply depots deep in the enemy rear. But it was the fighters that won command of the sky—planes now celebrated in aviation legend, like the German Fokker, Albatros and Pfalz, the British Sopwith Camel and Bristol, the French Nieuport and Spad. Except for the triplane Fokker, these were single-seat biplanes armed with one or two machine guns and capable of staying aloft for two hours. Eventually the best of them reached speeds of nearly 140 miles per hour and altitudes of over 20,000 feet.

On April 16, 1917, when the United States declared war on Germany, the Army Air Service (then part of the Signal Corps) had 55 aircraft, all of them trainers and all of them obsolete or obsolescent. Of its 131 officers, only 26 were fully trained pilots. Although American volunteers were serving in the air forces of France and Great Britain, no member of the U.S. Air Service had experienced aerial combat.

Congress quickly authorized the creation of a huge army, including a greatly expanded air service. There was talk of 20,000 U.S. airplanes darkening the skies over Europe. In the end, only 1,200 American-built (but British-designed) DH-4 reconnaissance bombers—the notorious "flying coffins"—reached the front. Most American pilots flew in French, British, and Italian planes.

On May 29, 1917, Major General John J. Pershing sailed from New York to establish in France the headquarters of the American Expeditionary Force that would follow the next year. His staff included a complement of hastily recruited clerks, interpreters, and chauffeurs. One of the latter was a tall, wiry 26-year-old racing-car driver named Eddie Rickenbacker.

Edward Vernon Rickenbacker was born on October 8, 1890, in Columbus, Ohio, the third of seven children of industrious German-speaking Swiss immigrants. When Eddie was 13, his father, a self-employed contractor, was killed in a construction accident. Eddie dropped out of the seventh grade, added a year to his age, and got a job in a glass factory working 12 hours a day, six days a week, for $3.50.

Fascinated by machinery, Eddie changed jobs several times until he landed in an automobile garage. There he mastered automobile engines with the help of a mail-order course in mechanical engineering from the International Correspondence School in Scranton, Pennsylvania. Soon he was working at the Frayer-Miller Company, an automobile manufacturer, where he received an advanced education in auto mechanics. Lee Frayer, president of the little company, believed in advertising his cars by racing them. In 1906, he took 15-year-old Eddie with him as riding mechanic in the Vanderbilt Cup race on Long Island. When Frayer accepted a position as chief engineer of the Columbus Buggy Company with the assignment to build a new car, he took Eddie, now 17, along as head of his testing department at $20 a week.

Still in his teens, Eddie Rickenbacker soon became an expert auto mechanic and a well-paid auto salesman. Auto racing followed, first as a means of promoting sales of his employers' cars, then as a career in itself. Beginning on dirt tracks at county fairs, he graduated to prestigious road races and, in 1911, for the first time raced in the Memorial Day 500 at the Indianapolis Speedway. By 1916 he was ranked third nationally among American auto racers and earned $60,000 in prize money.

In May 1917, while Eddie was preparing for the next Indianapolis race, a telephone call from an officer on General Pershing's staff summoned him to New York. Patriotic and adventurous, Rickenbacker promptly abandoned racing to be among the first Americans in France. Two days later he was a sergeant in the U.S. Army and on his way overseas.

In France, Rickenbacker often chauffeured Colonel William ("Billy") Mitchell, the chief air officer of the AEF. With Mitchell's influence, he was accepted for pilot training, although at 27 he was two years overage. After primary training from French instructors, he was commissioned a lieutenant and assigned to the advanced flying school at Issoudun—but as an engineering officer, not a student pilot. Nevertheless, he picked up what instruction he could and taught himself aerobatics while off duty. Eventually, the commander of the school—Major Carl "Tooey" Spaatz, a four-star general in World War II—granted Rickenbacker's insistent request to be assigned to gunnery school. In March 1918, now a trained combat pilot, Rickenbacker reported to the newly formed 94th Aero Pursuit Squadron at Toul, the first all-American squadron to go into action on the western front.

Toul was in a quiet sector where new American pilots could learn and practice their craft. The 94th was equipped with Nieuports that had been discarded by the French in favor of newer and faster Spads. The Nieuport could fly 122 miles an hour and could reach an altitude of 17,000 feet. Unfortunately, its upper wings tended to shed their fabric in a steep dive. The Nieuports of the 94th were soon decorated with the squadron's hat-in-the-ring insignia—Uncle Sam's top hat, starred and striped, inside a circle. In frontier days, the pilots recalled, throwing your hat in the ring was a challenge to a fight.

Among the squadron's 20 pilots were several veterans of the Lafayette Escadrille, a famous French unit composed of American volunteers. One of these was Major Raoul Lufbery, a top ace with 17 victories (enemy planes downed) to his credit. As soon as weather permitted, Lufbery led Rickenbacker and another novice on a patrol of their sector. To his great embarrassment, Rickenbacker became airsick, but before he could disgrace himself, the terror of German antiaircraft fire—"archy," in the pilots' slang—drove the nausea from his mind.

After their return from the otherwise uneventful patrol, Lufbery asked his two students if they had seen any other aircraft. They had not. Lufbery informed them that two formations of French Spads had passed nearby and that a formation of German Albatroses was approaching when they turned for home.

Learning to see other planes in the limitless sky was the beginning of Rickenbacker's combat education—an education he was fortunate to be able to pursue for another month before his first dogfight. From Lufbery he acquired a preference for flying alone rather than in formation, and he absorbed tactical lessons that only a veteran combat pilot could teach. Whenever he could, he practiced the aerobatics he would need in a fight, staying aloft until he became airsick. A crack mechanic who could diagnose an engine's problem from its sound, he personally checked his engine before each flight, and he supervised the loading of machine-gun

Rickenbacker behind the twin machine guns of his Spad, 1918.
(Smithsonian Institution Photo No. A4312A)

bullets into his ammunition belts to prevent his guns from jamming. "I was lucky that I lived long enough to learn," Rickenbacker recalled later. "Many a pilot went to his death before he gained the experience that would have kept him alive."

Rickenbacker's first dogfight—and his first victory—came on April 19, 1918. He surprised a new German Pfalz, dove onto its tail, and trained the sights of his two machine guns on the fleeing enemy. At 150 yards he pressed the triggers. Every fourth bullet was a tracer, and he could see the stream of fire pour into the Pfalz's tail. Pulling back on the stick, he raised the nose of his plane slightly. "It was like raising a garden hose," he recounted. The stream of bullets climbed the fuselage into the pilot's seat. The Pfalz swerved out of control and crashed.

Three weeks later, flying alone over German-held Metz, Rickenbacker spotted a formation of three German Albatroses beginning a flight south toward the front. Too late the Germans became aware of him as he dived on the rear plane. A 10-second burst of machine-gun fire sent the German plane out of control. Pulling out of his dive to face the other two Albatroses, Rickenbacker felt "a ripping, tearing crash" shaking his plane as the linen over the right upper wing was stripped away. The plane slipped into a tailspin, its controls useless. Seconds from death, Rickenbacker pulled open the throttle. Miraculously, the nose lifted and the plane became horizontal. With the Germans pursuing him as far as the front lines, Rickenbacker nursed his crippled plane homeward, through antiaircraft fire, to a crash landing on his own airfield. The Albatros was Rickenbacker's fifth victory. He was now an ace.

In the spring of 1918, a huge German offensive threatened Paris once again as in 1914. French and American troops halted the German advance at the Second Battle of the Marne in July, then counterattacked. The Germans fell back, leaving a 14-mile-deep salient (or bulge) in the French and American lines at St. Mihiel. The task of eliminating this salient was assigned to the newly organized U.S. First Army.

The American offensive against the St. Mihiel salient began on September 12. In support of the ground troops, Colonel Billy Mitchell directed 1,481 planes of all kinds, mostly borrowed from the British and French. It was the largest air fleet to engage in a single operation in World War I. By this time, the 94th had been reequipped with Spads, "the ultimate aircraft of the war," in Rickenbacker's opinion. Sturdy and reliable, the Spad could fly at 130 miles an hour and reach an altitude of 22,000 feet.

Heavy rain on September 12 drenched the attackers and grounded the air armada. At noon, Rickenbacker and a companion took off despite the rain. Crossing the front at 600 feet, they found the German army in full retreat, clogging the roads leading north. Spotting a battery of German artillery, the two Americans dived to the attack, strafing up and down the line. The column was thrown into wild confusion. Horses plunged and broke away. Drivers and gunners took refuge in the trees.

The next day, flying alone above the German lines, Rickenbacker had his first encounter with the Flying Circus, the dreaded German squadron whose pilots included such famous aces as Manfred von Richthofen, Ernst Udet, and Hermann Goering. With the sun at his back, and enjoying superior altitude, Rickenbacker spotted four German Fokkers in diamond formation. He dived on the rear plane and sent it crashing to earth. When the other three Fokkers turned on him, Rickenbacker recognized the distinctive red noses of the Flying Circus. Outnumbered, his only thought was escape. He exhausted his repertoire of aerobatics, but still the Fokkers whipped around him, trying to get him in their gun sights. At last he saw an opportunity to escape. With his motor wide open and the nose of his plane pointed straight down, he dived through the melee and raced for home, leaving the Fokkers in the distance.

On September 24, Rickenbacker was promoted to captain and appointed commander of the hat-in-the-ring squadron. Of the original 20 pilots who had formed the 94th in March, only he and two others remained. Rickenbacker had not been popular in the squadron at first. From a working-class background, he was uneducated, cocky, profane—in short, he was not a gentleman. The others were generally well-bred college men from upper-class families. But in time he won the respect and even the affection of his fellow pilots. If he was not the fanciest flier, he was certainly a ferocious fighter. They appreciated his resolve never to ask them to do anything he would not do himself.

Determined to make the 94th the best squadron in the AEF and to set a personal example for his pilots, Rickenbacker celebrated his promotion by going up alone the next morning and single-handedly attacking a formation of five Fokker pursuit planes escorting two observation craft, shooting down one of each—a "doubleheader" for which he received the congressional Medal of Honor in 1930. Rickenbacker was pleased about the "good effect" his feat had on the other pilots.

The final American campaign of the war, the Meuse–Argonne offensive, began on September 26. Pershing now had a million men under his command, and Billy Mitchell, now a brigadier general, had massed 800 aircraft. But the Germans held superior positions and resisted stubbornly. After initial successes, the drive slowed. Throughout October, the fighting was bitter. Only in early November did the German collapse heralding the end of the war begin.

In this offensive, the 94th was assigned the task of destroying German observation balloons—a dangerous mission, since the balloons were heavily defended by antiaircraft fire from the ground and by German fighters in the air. "Those were hectic days," Rickenbacker recalled. "I put in six or seven hours flying time each day. I would come down, gulp a cup of coffee while the mechanics refueled the plane and patched the bullet holes, and take off again."

One day, while pursuing a German plane that had just destroyed an American balloon, Rickenbacker was taken by surprise by two

Fokkers on his tail. They would expect him to dive, he calculated, so instead he twisted upward in a corkscrew maneuver called a "chandelle." But two more Fokkers were waiting above him. All four had the red noses of the Flying Circus. Rickenbacker zig-zagged and sideslipped, but the Fokkers clung to him. Then, for a split second, he saw that one of the Fokkers below him was vulnerable. He dived, firing his machine guns ahead of the Fokker, which flew into the stream of fire. Its gas tank exploded, and the Fokker went down in flames. Instead of attacking, the other three Fokkers turned for home. Rickenbacker pursued them into German territory. One Fokker fell behind, and Rickenbacker shot it down at an altitude of only 1,000 feet. Only then did he become aware that ground fire was flashing all around him. He turned and flew for home with victories 18 and 19.

At 11 A.M. on November 11, 1918, the war ended. The 94th Aero Pursuit Squadron led all American units with 70 victories, and Rickenbacker led all American pilots with 26—22 planes and four balloons. He was America's "ace of aces."

Rickenbacker returned to the United States in 1919 a hero. Assigned to promote the sale of Liberty Bonds, he toured the country, enduring parades, banquets, and speeches. He wrote an exciting account of his wartime experiences in a book called *Fighting the Flying Circus* (1919). And then Captain Rickenbacker was discharged.

The hero was 30 years old. Pondering his future, he decided he had two goals. One was to build a superior automobile that incorporated all he had learned as a racing driver; the other was to promote aviation. (Curiously, Rickenbacker never earned either a driver's license or a pilot's license.) After working briefly for General Motors, in 1922 he became vice president of the Rickenbacker Motor Company, which produced the first American automobile with four-wheel brakes. But the small company was no match for the giant auto companies, and in 1927 the Rickenbacker Motor Company went bankrupt.

Rickenbacker rejoined General Motors in 1929 as a sales executive but was soon transferred to the company's aviation divisions, and in 1934 he was appointed general manager of GM-owned Eastern Air Lines. When GM put the airline up for sale in 1938, Rickenbacker—who never lacked rich and influential friends—succeeded in raising the necessary $3.5 million. He became owner and president of the airline.

In his first year as manager of Eastern Air Lines, Rickenbacker produced a profit—the first in the history of the fledgling industry. For 25 years thereafter, Eastern continued to be profitable, despite intense competition and Rickenbacker's adamant refusal to accept government subsidies. It also grew from a small and unsuccessful carrier—the "ugly duckling" of the industry—into one of the nation's premier airlines.

During World War II, Rickenbacker was called back to his country's service. Sent to inspect air bases around the world, he visited every theater of the war. On October 29, 1942, he left Honolulu in a B-17 Flying Fortress on a flight to New Guinea. The first stop was to be Canton Island, 1,800 miles southwest of Hawaii. But the plane missed its destination and ditched in the trackless Pacific. Rickenbacker and seven companions escaped the sinking plane in rubber rafts. Although he was the only civilian in the group, 52-year-old Rickenbacker took command. His iron will kept the survivors from despair while they drifted for 23 days, subsisting on rainwater, a seagull, and some fish. Back home, the nation mourned the hero's death. But on November 13 a patrolling American plane spotted the rafts. Rickenbacker and six other survivors were rescued. After two weeks spent recuperating, he continued his tour. Later he wrote an account of his Pacific ordeal called *Seven Came Through* (1943).

After the war, Rickenbacker returned to Eastern Airlines. He resigned as president in 1959, and in 1963 he retired as director and chairman of the board. In 1967 he published an autobiography titled simply *Rickenbacker*. He died on July 23, 1973.

Overaged and with only a sixth-grade education, Rickenbacker was not typical of American pilots in the First World War. But he contributed more than his share to the legend that these gallant young men created—a legend that, during the 1920s and 1930s, inspired a host of boys' adventure books and motion pictures like *Wings* (1928), *Hell's Angels* (1930), and *Dawn Patrol* (1930). The legend was not untrue. The gentleman pilots in their goggles and fleece-lined flying suits, trailing white silk scarves from their open cockpits, whirling in lethal dogfights in the numbing cold of 15,000 feet, were indeed brave men who knew that their life expectancy was brief. Rickenbacker may have been more careful and skilled than the others. He was certainly luckier. He lived.

But Rickenbacker's real significance for aviation was not his feats of heroism as a fighter pilot but his constructive work in commercial aviation. He had an unfashionable faith in the future of commercial aviation, and particularly in the future of Eastern Air Lines. As president of Eastern, he showed for the first time that a passenger-carrying airline could be profitable—and without government subsidies. From a handful of airplanes and a few hundred employees serving the New York–Miami route in 1935, Eastern under his direction grew into an industry giant. When he retired in 1963, the airline served 113 cities in 26 states, Canada, Bermuda, Mexico, and Puerto Rico. Its 173 aircraft carried more than 10 million passengers that year. "Captain Eddie" was a tough, dictatorial manager who provided no-frills service. He refused to compete with his rivals on cabin decor or in-flight amenities like filet mignon dinners. Instead, he stressed safety, reliability, and courtesy—and the public responded with confidence. Confidence is the essential element in commercial aviation.

Chronology

October 8, 1890	born in Columbus, Ohio
1903	his father dies and Eddie goes to work at $3.50 per week
1906	gets a job at Frayer-Miller Automobile Co., rides in first auto race as a mechanic
1916	his racing team wins seven of 13 major races; Rickenbacker ranks third among American auto racers
1917	enlists in U.S. Army as chauffeur on the staff of General John J. Pershing, goes to France, trains as a pilot
1918	shoots down 22 German planes, four balloons, becomes the U.S. "ace of aces"
1919	returns to the United States a hero
1922	becomes vice president of Rickenbacker Motor Company, which goes bankrupt in 1927
1927	buys Indianapolis Speedway, which he holds until 1945

1934	appointed general manager of General Motors-owned Eastern Air Lines
1938	becomes owner and president of Eastern Air Lines
1941	survives crash of Eastern plane in Atlanta, Georgia
1942	survives 23 days on raft in Pacific after ditching of the B-17 carrying him to New Guinea
1959	resigns as president of Eastern Air Lines
1963	retires as chairman of Eastern Air Lines
July 23, 1973	dies in Zurich, Switzerland

Further Reading

Books by Edward V. Rickenbacker

Fighting the Flying Circus. New York: Frederick A. Stokes Co., 1919; republished by Doubleday in 1965. A vivid account of the adventures of the World War I "ace of aces."

Rickenbacker. Englewood Cliffs, N.J.: Prentice-Hall, 1967. The autobiography of a tough but sentimental man whose religious faith sustained him through many harrowing experiences.

Seven Came Through. Garden City, N.Y.: Doubleday, 1943. Rickenbacker's compelling account of 23 days adrift on the Pacific Ocean during World War II.

Books About Edward V. Rickenbacker

Farr, Finis. *Rickenbacker's Luck: An American Life*. Boston: Houghton Mifflin, 1979. A frank, candid biography, more concerned with Rickenbacker's business and political activities than with his career as an auto racer and pilot.

Serling, Robert J. *From the Captain to the Colonel: An Informal History of Eastern Air Lines*. New York: Dial Press, 1980. About half of this chatty, anecdotal history is devoted to the Rickenbacker era at Eastern.

Charles A. Lindbergh

Charles Lindbergh with the Spirit of St. Louis *at Curtiss Field, Long Island, in May 1927 before his Paris flight.*
(Smithsonian Institution Photo No. 87-8992)

*M*orning dawns gray, misty, dripping. Rain fell all day yesterday and through most of the night. At the western end of the sodden runway at Roosevelt Field on Long Island sits a plain, silver, high-wing monoplane, its single engine idling. It is the *Spirit of St. Louis*, and its pilot, a tall, lean young man dressed in army breeches and a tight woolen sweater, stands beside it, weighing a decision that could mean life or death.

He is Charles Lindbergh, age 25. A week ago he was an unknown airmail pilot from St. Louis. Today he is the focus of the nation's sensation-hungry press. His decision will make headlines across the country, around the world.

He has had only a few minutes' sleep in the last 24 hours, and now he faces a 36-hour flight. But the decision that confronts him is whether to attempt a takeoff. The little plane holds 450 gallons of fuel in its nose, fuselage, and wing tanks—more than it has ever lifted before. Its tires, greased to prevent mud from sticking to them, bulge under the weight. Tested at full throttle, the 200-horsepower Wright Whirlwind engine has turned the plane's propeller at a rate 40 revolutions per minute slower than expected because of the muggy weather. And instead of the desired headwind, a tail wind now blows lightly. Puddles glisten on the unpaved, rain-soaked runway. Although it is a mile long, the runway may not be long enough for the overloaded plane, and at its end there is a line of telephone wires.

But for the first time in a week the weather reports are favorable. Although Roosevelt Field is shrouded in mist, the skies have cleared over New England, Newfoundland, and the North Atlantic. How long they will remain clear no one can say.

Still undecided, Lindbergh pulls on his heavy flying suit, his helmet and his goggles, and climbs into the plane's cramped cabin with two canteens of water and a bag of sandwiches. He has no forward vision because of the fuselage gas tank but must lean out of the open side windows to look ahead. He feels the cockpit quiver, hears the sharp explosions from the exhaust pipes. He can still cancel the takeoff and no one will criticize him for it.

The decision is not a logical one. It is determined by experience and intuition. The conviction surges through him that the wheels *will* leave the ground, that the plane *will* rise above the wires at the end of the runway. The decision is made.

"I buckle my safety belt," Lindbergh later recounted, "pull goggles down over my eyes, turn to the men at the blocks, and nod. Frozen figures leap to action. A yank on the ropes—the wheels are free. I brace myself against the left side of the cockpit, sight along the edge of the runway, and ease the throttle wide open. Action brings confidence and relief.

"The plane creeps heavily forward. Several men are pushing on wing struts to help it start—pushing so hard I'm afraid the struts will buckle.

"The *Spirit of St. Louis* feels more like an overloaded truck than an airplane. The tires rut through mud as though they really were on truck wheels. Even the breath of wind is pressing me down.

"Gradually, the speed increases. The engine's snarl sounds inadequate and weak. There's none of the spring forward that always before preceded the takeoff into air—no lightness of wing, no excess power. The stick wobbles loosely from side to side, and slipstream puts hardly any pressure against rudder. Nothing about my plane has the magic quality of flight. But men begin stumbling off from the wing struts. We're going faster.

"A hundred yards of runway passes. The last man drops off the struts. The stick's wobbling changes to lurching motion as ailerons protest unevenness of surface.

"Pace quickens. Turf becomes a blur. The tail skid lifts off ground. I feel the load shifting from wheels to wings. But the runway's slipping by quickly. The halfway mark is just ahead, and I have nothing like flying speed.

"The halfway mark streaks past. I pull the stick back firmly, and *the wheels leave the ground*. The wheels touch again. I ease the stick forward. Almost flying speed, and nearly 2000 feet of field ahead. A shallow pool on the runway. Water spews up from the tires. A wing drops, lifts as I shove aileron against it. The entire plane trembles from the shock. Off again. Right wing low. Pull it up. Ease back onto the runway. Another pool, water drumming on the fabric. The next hop's longer. I let the wheels touch once more—lightly, a last bow to earth.

"The *Spirit of St. Louis* takes herself off the next time. Full flying speed. The controls taut, alive, straining—and still a thousand feet to the web of telephone wires. I keep the nose down, climbing slowly, each second gaining speed. Five feet, twenty, forty—wires flash by underneath. Twenty feet to spare!"

The *Spirit of St. Louis* heads north on the great circle route—the shortest distance between two points on the surface of a sphere—to Paris, 3,600 miles and 36 hours away.

It is 7:42 A.M., Friday, May 20, 1927.

Charles A. Lindbergh Jr. was born on February 4, 1902, in the home of his mother's parents in Detroit, Michigan. His father was the son of Swedish immigrants who, in the 1860s, had carved out a farm in the woodlands of eastern Minnesota. In 1902 the senior Lindbergh was a prosperous attorney in the lumbering town of Little Falls, Minnesota. Stolid and taciturn, he had no intimate friends, but he enjoyed a reputation for rocklike integrity. In 1906 his neighbors elected him to the first of five terms in the U.S. House of Representatives, where, as a Republican of independent mind, he denounced the Wall Street "money trust" and opposed U.S. intervention in the First World War. Accused of socialism and disloyalty, he was defeated in a race for the U.S. Senate in 1916 and defeated again in 1918 when he ran for governor of Minnesota.

Charles's mother, a graduate of the University of Michigan and Columbia University, had come to Little Falls to teach science in the local high school. Aloof and superior, she was not popular in the town. Her life was devoted entirely to her son.

The Lindberghs lived on a farm on the west bank of the Mississippi River two miles south of Little Falls. Except for winters in Washington when his father was a congressman, Charles grew up out of doors, shooting, hunting, swimming, and boating. Good in science and mechanical drawing, he was otherwise an average student, less interested in school than in his father's automobiles and in a motorcycle he acquired as a teenager.

Like his parents, Charles was self-sufficient and solitary, with no close friends. He had little empathy for others, and his sense of humor was manifested in the sadistic practical jokes that, as a young man, he played on his associates. From his mother he acquired an unpleasant censoriousness, passing harsh judgments on others who were not as serious-minded as himself. And he was extremely serious-minded. He did not smoke, drink, gamble, dance, or socialize with girls. At one point he drew up a list of 65 "character factors" and graded himself daily on each. One of these was courage. Even as a boy, whenever he felt fear he would confront it directly and strive to overcome it. In some cases his triumphs over fear were achieved by feats—on his motorcycle or, later, in the air—that seemed to others to be wildly reckless but that he had carefully analyzed and planned beforehand.

In 1920, at age 18, Charles Lindbergh stood six feet three inches tall. He was extremely thin but physically hard; handsome, with tousled blond hair, direct blue eyes, and a boyish grin; poorly educated; severe in his judgments; self-possessed and self-determined; and intensely private—in every respect the very opposite of the frivolous, partying and hedonistic "flaming youth" of the new Jazz Age.

That year, more to please his mother than himself, he enrolled at the University of Wisconsin to study mechanical engineering. His mother moved to Madison to be with him. But he found student life childish, and in March 1922, after only three semesters, he told his mother that he had decided to leave college and become an aviator. Devastated, she replied only, "You must lead your own life."

Lindbergh had seen an advertisement for a flying school conducted by the Nebraska Aircraft Corporation, manufacturer of the Lincoln Standard airplane, at its factory in Lincoln, Nebraska. When he reached Lincoln in April 1922, he discovered that the school consisted of one plane, one instructor, and one student—

himself. For his $500 tuition fee, he was permitted to learn what he could about aircraft design and construction on the factory floor and was given irregular flying lessons by a burned- out wartime pilot. Lindbergh had completed eight hours of instruction, but had not yet soloed, when the company sold the training plane, effectively liquidating the school.

The plane's purchaser was a local pilot who planned to go on a barnstorming tour in June. Lindbergh persuaded the pilot to take him along as an unpaid mechanic and helper. In those days, barnstorming was one of the few ways pilots could support their hobby. In two-seater, open-cockpit planes, barnstorming pilots flew throughout the rural areas of America's Midwest, South, and West, buzzing small towns to announce their arrival and then landing in a nearby field or pasture. When a small crowd collected, the pilot would attempt to sell rides for $5 apiece. It was a gypsy life. Pilots carried their few personal belongings in duffel bags or in the deep pockets of their coveralls. Often they slept at night on the ground under the wings of their planes. Earnings were small, and when the weather was bad or when it turned chilly in the autumn there were no customers at all. Occasionally a pilot would discover that he was close behind another barnstormer who had "creamed" most of the business, sometimes at discount rates.

If a barnstormer could put on some kind of aerial show, he could attract larger crowds and more potential customers. Aerobatics was one such crowd-attracting device. Doing stunts was another. Lindbergh became a stuntman, performing daring feats of wing walking and, later, parachute jumping for the barnstorming pilots he accompanied. Leaflets announcing the arrival of "Daredevil Lindbergh" would be dropped from the plane over a small town, and people would flock to see the free show.

In April 1923, at Americus, Georgia, Lindbergh bought his own airplane. It was a war-surplus but newly assembled Jenny, the famous army trainer, with a 90-horsepower engine; it was capable of flying 60 or 70 miles per hour—if there was no headwind. It cost $500. After one accompanied flight in the new craft, Lindbergh soloed at last. A week later he took off for a barnstorming tour through the South and West.

He was now a full-fledged member of the fraternity of gypsy fliers—men with no particular homes other than their airplanes, solitary men wandering over vast expanses of the country, living hand to mouth on the meager proceeds of barnstorming, surviving frequent forced landings and occasional crackups, and meeting their fellow pilots only on stopovers at established airfields or at infrequent air shows and races. For the moment, this was all that Lindbergh wanted to do. He loved flying and the solitary life of the gypsy flier. Of course, he believed that there was a future in aviation, but in 1923 that future was hidden from view.

Early in 1924 Lindbergh applied for an appointment as a cadet in the Army Air Service. The army afforded valuable technical training and a chance to fly modern airplanes. Lindbergh was accepted, and he reported to Brooks Field in San Antonio, Texas, on March 15, 1924. The 104 new cadets received their primary training in the familiar Jennies, now equipped with 150-horsepower Hispano-Suiza engines in place of the old 90-horsepower OX-5s. In addition, there were intensive ground courses in such subjects as aerodynamics, navigation, radio, and military law.

Only 33 cadets successfully completed primary training. Lindbergh came in second in his class. Then it was on to Kelly Field 10 miles away for advance training, which was conducted in De Havillands, the Army's observation plane. Later, cadets could specialize in one of four types of combat flying: pursuit, attack, observation, and bombardment. Lindbergh chose pursuit, and trained in the Army's SE-5 Scout, a single-engine biplane with a speed of 115 miles per hour. A few days before graduation, Lindbergh's plane and another fighter, climbing out of a diving attack in close formation, collided, their wings locking. Both pilots bailed out and survived. It was the first time that anyone had survived a midair collision. It was the first time, too, that Lindbergh's name appeared in a New York newspaper.

Despite the accident, Lindbergh graduated first in his class at Kelly Field. Of the 104 men who had reported to Brooks Field the year before, only 18 were commissioned second lieutenants and awarded their wings on March 15, 1925. Most, including Lindbergh, promptly resigned from the army, although they remained members of the Air Service Reserve Corps. Lindbergh would later join the Missouri National Guard, where he would be promoted to captain.

From Kelly Field, Lindbergh went north to St. Louis. Two brothers, William and Frank Robertson, wartime pilots and owners of the Robertson Aircraft Corporation, based at Lambert Field in St. Louis, had promised him a job. The Robertsons had met Lindbergh during his barnstorming days and had been impressed by his ability as a flier. In 1925 they were bidding for the airmail route between St. Louis and Chicago, and if they got it, Lindbergh

Charles A. Lindbergh

was to be their chief pilot. The U.S. Post Office Department had begun flying the mail in 1918. By 1920 it had established a transcontinental route linking New York with San Francisco, with "feeder" routes from Washington to New York and from St. Louis and Minneapolis to Chicago. But in 1925 the Kelly Act transferred airmail service to private hands as a way of subsidizing the development of commercial aviation. Aviation companies with sufficient resources bid for various routes, which were awarded by the postmaster general. Eventually, the Robertsons, with a fleet of 14 De Havillands, won the St. Louis–Chicago route.

As chief pilot, Lindbergh hired two other army pilots and selected nine emergency landing fields between St. Louis and Chicago. On April 15, 1926, he inaugurated the new Robertson service with a flight from Chicago to St. Louis in the morning and a return flight to Chicago in the afternoon, a distance of 285 miles each way, with stops at Peoria and Springfield. During the summer months, flying the mail proved routine and uneventful, but fall brought early darkness and turbulent weather. Forced landings were frequent, and twice—in September and November 1926—Lindbergh had to bail out of disabled planes in darkness and fog.

In 1926, Raymond Orteig, a French hotel owner, renewed his offer, first made in 1919, of $25,000 for the first nonstop flight in either direction between France and the United States, the competition to be administered by the National Aeronautics Association in Washington. By 1926, in contrast to 1919, aviation had progressed to the point where such a flight was feasible—just barely. Airplanes large enough to carry the necessary fuel, and engines reliable enough to make the distance, had been developed. Some of the world's foremost aviators announced plans to compete for the prize. Most planned to use multiengine planes with crews of two to four. René Fonck, a renowned French ace of World War I, intended to make a west–east flight with a crew of four in a trimotor ship designed by Igor Sikorsky. U.S. Navy commander Richard E. Byrd, who had recently flown over the North Pole, planned to make the crossing in a trimotor Fokker, also with a crew of four. Another French aviation hero, Charles Nungesser, was preparing to make an east–west flight with only a navigator.

News of the competition excited Lindbergh. The mortal risk involved in a transatlantic flight only made the challenge more irresistible to him. He believed that the flight could be best accomplished with the simplest possible elements—an airplane capable of carrying sufficient fuel, a single engine, an absolute minimum of instruments and equipment, and a crew of one, the pilot. The more elaborate the plane, he reasoned, the more there would be to go wrong. In Lindbergh's scheme, the crucial element was the pilot. The flight might take as long as 40 hours. Could any pilot, unaided, fly his ship for 40 hours without relief, without sleep? Lindbergh never doubted that he could.

Lindbergh's view of the problem was partially confirmed on September 20, 1926, when Fonck attempted to take off for Paris from Roosevelt Field, Long Island, in his trimotor Sikorsky biplane. The plane never left the ground, and crashed at the end of the runway. Two of the four men aboard were killed. Fonck announced that he would try again.

Lindbergh's plan would cost only a fraction of what the other contestants were spending, but even that was more than he could afford. He had $2,000 of his own to risk in the venture. For the rest, he approached a number of St. Louis businessmen with the argument that a successful flight by a resident of St. Louis, financed by St. Louis businessmen, and in a plane bearing the name of St. Louis, would advance the city's reputation as an aviation center. Lindbergh proved persuasive, and soon he had pledges totaling $15,000. His own $2,000 was the largest single contribution.

Finding an airplane proved more difficult, especially when Lindbergh made it clear that he would fly alone. Fokker, the Wright Company, and others refused to sell him a plane, fearing that their reputations would be jeopardized by association with this unknown daredevil. However, a small company in San Diego, California, called Ryan Airlines seemed positively eager to provide a plane for him. In February 1927 Lindbergh traveled to San Diego. The men at Ryan were young and enthusiastic, eager to build him a plane to his specifications—a range of 4,000 miles, a Wright J-5 Whirlwind engine with a top speed of 130 miles per hour, all within 60 days. The price was $10,580, excluding instruments.

For the next two months, Lindbergh worked on the factory floor beside the Ryan designers and mechanics, watching the craft develop and planning his course. It was a trim plane 9 feet 8 inches high and 27 feet 8 inches long, with an oversized, square- tipped wing. In effect, the stripped-down plane was a flying gas tank. Instruments were minimal—compasses, altimeter, speed and turning indicators, and temperature gauges. There was no radio, and though Lindbergh decided to take a rubber life raft he did not expect to carry a parachute.

The finished plane, christened the *Spirit of St. Louis*, made its maiden flight at San Diego on April 28, 1927. There were further tests during the next two weeks. Meanwhile, the other contestants were not faring well. On April 16, Byrd's trimotor Fokker, *America*, crashed on a test flight at Teterboro Airport in New Jersey and had to undergo extensive repairs. On April 26, Lieutenant Commander Noel Davis and his copilot, testing a trimotor Keystone Pathfinder biplane, the *American Legion*, were killed in a crash at Langley Field, Virginia. And on May 8, the French ace Charles Nungesser and a navigator took off from Le Bourget airfield in Paris in a single-engine Levasseur biplane—only to disappear over the Atlantic.

On May 10, 1927, at 3:55 P.M., Lindbergh took off from San Diego in the *Spirit of St. Louis* for a nonstop flight to St. Louis, where he arrived at 8:20 A.M. on May 11. His was the first night flight over the Rocky Mountains, the longest nonstop solo on record, and the fastest time from the West Coast to St. Louis. On May 12, at 8:13 A.M., he left St. Louis, arriving at Curtiss Field on Long Island at 5:33 P.M. His actual flying time from coast to coast, 21 hours and 30 minutes, was five and a half hours faster than the existing transcontinental record.

Two other planes were on Long Island preparing for the transatlantic flight. At nearby Roosevelt Field, Byrd's *America*, its repairs completed, was being readied for takeoff. At Curtiss Field, a plane designed by Giuseppe Bellanca and piloted by Clarence Chamberlin was prevented from taking off only by a court order initiated by a disgruntled crewman. In England, France, and Italy, other pilots were reportedly preparing for the transatlantic flight.

A week of bad weather kept all three planes grounded. Byrd generously invited Lindbergh and Chamberlin to use Roosevelt Field, whose runway had been extended at his own expense. Not until May 19 was there a break in the weather. Restless and eager to beat the others into the air, Lindbergh ordered his plane towed from Curtiss to Roosevelt Field during the night. At dawn, after a sleepless night, he made his decision to take off.

From Roosevelt Field, Lindbergh's course led across Long Island Sound, Connecticut, Rhode Island, and eastern Massachusetts. He flew his heavy plane very low, barely a hundred feet off the ground. In the flight's third hour he passed near Plymouth, Massachusetts, and was over open ocean for the first time in his life. For two hours he was out of sight of land. His legs became stiff and cramped, but he knew the pain would eventually subside into numbness. In the flight's fifth hour he crossed the low, grassy coast of Nova Scotia at a point only six miles from his planned course. Across Nova Scotia and Cape Breton Island, and he was again over open ocean, but this time the surface was glaring white—an ice field. He began to feel dangerously tired, unable to keep his eyes open without conscious effort. Over Newfoundland he deviated 90 miles from his course in order to pass low over St. John's, then headed out to sea. Now North America was behind him, Ireland 2,000 miles ahead. Below him, in the 12th hour of the flight, icebergs gleamed lustrous white against the dark water of the North Atlantic.

Night rushed over the little plane; fog and haze shrouded the sea and rose up to envelop it. Lindbergh climbed to escape. Above the haze, he could see a few bright stars in the black sky. The luminous dials of his instruments stared at him with ghostlike eyes. At 10,000 feet the air was bitterly cold, and he buttoned his flying suit. By the dim starlight he discovered that he was flying among cloud mountains—huge pillars of cloud that towered far above him. Unable to fly over them, he plunged into a mountainous thunderhead directly in his path. Blackness and turbulence swallowed the plane. Ice formed on wings and struts. Alarmed, he turned slowly to escape the thunderhead in the direction by which he had entered, then resumed his eastward course. Now he was careful to fly around the cloud pillars, weaving through narrow canyons between tremendous, fantastic shapes that loomed all around him.

The moon rose, flooding the cloud landscape with unearthly silver light. Suddenly the air in the slipstream that passed the open window of the cockpit became warm. He had passed over the Labrador Current and was now flying above the Gulf Stream. Ice disappeared from the struts. The cockpit became warm, and he loosened his flying suit. In the flight's 18th hour, the sky brightened with the promise of sunrise. This was the third morning since he had slept, and now he fought sleep desperately. His eyes closed despite every effort to keep them open. He was grateful for the very instability of his plane—the slightest relaxation on the controls caused the plane to climb or turn, forcing him back from the edge of sleep.

When morning came, he descended to examine the ocean. He found a heavy sea running, streaked with foam raised by gale-force winds from the northwest. He had had a tail wind all night. In the flight's 22nd hour, flying through fog and mist, he became aware that he was sleeping with his eyes open, helplessly passing in and out of consciousness. Behind him, the plane's fuselage seemed to be filled with ghostly forms, transparent, moving; in his trance he felt no surprise. Emerging from a cloud, he saw a coastline with cliffs, hills, trees paralleling his course. But this was only a fog island, a mirage. It was the flight's 24th hour, and for the first time he doubted his ability to make it. The realization that death was at hand reenergized his body's senses. He shook himself awake, put his face out the window into the slipstream and gulped the air. The crisis passed. He was not threatened by sleep again.

In the flight's 27th hour he spied a fleet of fishing boats on the ocean's surface. He banked down for a closer inspection. There was no sign of life on the first boat. On the second, a man's head emerged from a porthole. Lindbergh shut off his engine and glided low over the boat. "Which way is Ireland?" he shouted. There was no response. He climbed again, confident that land was near but with no sure sense of where he was. Then there was land, low on the horizon to his left, no mirage this time. He flew to it and found himself over Dingle Bay on the southwest coast of Ireland, almost exactly on course and two and a half hours ahead of schedule. People in village streets waved to him. Exultant, he felt he had never before seen anything as beautiful as the Irish countryside.

Southeastward he flew on, across St. George's Channel, across Cornwall in western England, over Plymouth and out over the English Channel. He crossed the French coast at Deauville. Night came on. In the darkness, a glow on the eastern horizon heralded the approach of Paris. The city rose over the edge of the earth to meet him. He circled the Eiffel Tower, then looked for Le Bourget, missed it, returned and found it. This was a new airport for him, and he descended carefully, circling, finally touching down in the dark. It was 10:24 P.M., Saturday, May 21. He had been airborne for 33 ½ hours.

As he taxied toward a lighted area, he became aware that the darkness before him was alive. A vast crowd was racing toward the plane, like the edge of an advancing tide, and thousands of voices were shouting "Lindbergh! Lindbergh!"

Lindbergh's perilous flight had been followed anxiously on two continents. His safe arrival in Paris unleashed a storm of celebration rarely seen before. He was carried from his plane on the shoulders of the French crowd. The next morning he awoke in the

51

American embassy to find a huge crowd out front, hundreds of reporters and photographers at the gates, and heaps of congratulatory cables and telegrams from all over the world. For the next two weeks, in Paris, Brussels, and London, he was cheered, feted, and decorated. On June 4, he sailed for home aboard the U.S. cruiser *Memphis*, flagship of the American European fleet.

The *Memphis* brought him to Alexandria, Virginia, and for two days he was the center of celebrations in Washington. President Calvin Coolidge awarded him the Distinguished Flying Cross, and he was the guest of the Coolidges overnight while crowds waited in the street for a glimpse of him. He was promoted to colonel in the reserves, and later Congress awarded him the Medal of Honor. The Smithsonian Institution asked to keep the *Spirit of St. Louis* when he was finished with it.

In New York there were four days of celebrations, beginning with the traditional ticker-tape parade, watched by the largest crowd in the city's history. From New York he flew to St. Louis, where the reception was no less enthusiastic. On June 22 he went to Dayton, Ohio to pay his respects to Orville Wright. A month later he embarked in the *Spirit of St. Louis* on a tour of 82 cities in all 48 states that did not end until October 23. Everywhere, there were parades, banquets, cheering throngs. The tour, sponsored by the Guggenheim Fund for the Promotion of Aeronautics and the U.S. Department of Commerce, was intended, among other things, to demonstrate the safety and punctuality of professional flying, so Lindbergh made a point of adhering precisely to schedule. His performance was flawless. Earlier in the summer he had written a short autobiography and account of the Paris flight titled *We* that was published on July 27. the book sold 190,000 copies in eight weeks.

In Washington, Lindbergh had met Dwight Morrow, a partner in the banking firm of J. P. Morgan and the newly appointed U.S. ambassador to Mexico. Morrow thought that a flight by Lindbergh to Mexico would improve the troubled relations between the two countries. Lindbergh left Washington's Bolling Field in the *Spirit of St. Louis* on December 13, 1927, reaching Mexico City 27 hours and 15 minutes later. He was lost for nearly three hours over Mexico, and the anxious crowds that awaited his arrival in the Mexican capital were relieved as well as enthusiastic. Five days later Lindbergh left Mexico City and toured 14 Latin American countries and the Canal Zone before returning home.

In June 1928 Lindbergh was appointed chairman of the technical committee of Transcontinental Air Transport (TAT), the predecessor of Trans World Airlines (TWA). His job was to survey new air routes, locate and equip air fields, and select and test new airplanes for the expanding carrier. Thereafter TAT advertised itself as "The Lindbergh Line." In January 1929 he became a technical consultant for Pan American Airways as well. Both jobs were part-time, and there was no conflict of interest because TWA was developing domestic routes and Pan American was interested in flying overseas.

In March 1929 Lindbergh married Anne Morrow, a daughter of Dwight Morrow. A recent graduate of Smith College, shy and diffident, she seemed the very opposite of the heroic aviator. But Lindbergh taught her to fly, and she mastered navigation and radio operation as well. She even qualified as a glider pilot when he did. Anne flew with him on his survey work, including a record-breaking nonstop transcontinental flight on Easter Sunday 1930 to demonstrate the speed and safety of high-altitude flight. Together they also located archaeological sites from the air in Arizona, Mexico, and Central America.

For Pan American in 1931 the Lindberghs flew a new plane called the *Sirius*, a low-wing Lockheed monoplane equipped with pontoons, on a dramatic flight from New York to China along the great circle route. The flight took them from New York to the Arctic coast of Canada and Alaska, then down through the Bering Strait to Siberia and Japan and finally to Nanking, China. They returned to the United States by ship, and Anne wrote about the adventure in *North to the Orient* (1935). Unable to get permission from the Soviet Union and Japan, Pan American never used the great circle route pioneered by the Lindberghs. Instead, with the encouragement of the U.S. Navy, it developed a mid-Pacific route with stops at Midway, Wake, Guam, Manila, and Hong Kong. In 1935, the Pan American "China Clippers" began regular transpacific service over this route.

The Lindberghs made another celebrated flight for Pan Am in 1933 to survey alternative passenger routes to Europe. One was the great circle route that Charles had flown in 1927, another was a northern route by way of Greenland, and a third was a southern route via the Azores. The *Sirius*, now equipped with a new 710-horsepower engine and all the latest navigation equipment, left New York on July 9, 1933. After visiting 14 European countries, the Lindberghs flew down the west coast of Africa, crossing the South Atlantic from Gambia to Brazil, a distance of 1,800 miles. They returned to New York on December 19, having flown more than 29,000 miles. The

Lindbergh in a Pan American Airways trimotor Fokker VII in Havana,
February 1929.
(Pan American World Airways)

flight was widely acclaimed as a milestone for aviation. The *Sirius*
was placed on exhibition at New York's American Museum of
Natural History. Anne Lindbergh's *Listen! The Wind* (1938) de-
scribed the portion of their flight between Africa and Brazil.

Charles Lindbergh's work for TAT and Pan Am left him time for
other interests. He became involved in the work of Alexis Carrel,
a French Nobel Prize–winning surgeon who was working at the
Rockefeller Institute in New York City on organ transplants.
Lindbergh invented a perfusion pump that made it possible to
keep organs alive outside the body. He also took an interest in the
work of rocket experimenter Robert H. Goddard of Clark University, and persuaded the Guggenheim Foundation to support it.

The 1927 Paris flight decisively altered Lindbergh's life. Although the public's hysterical adulation gradually subsided, its
interest in him did not. Wherever the hero went, he was the focus
of the curious, the boorish, the worshipful. He came to loathe his
insatiable admirers. Worst of all was the press, whose intrusive-
ness and untruthful reporting maddened him.

Charles A. Lindbergh

Besides making him a celebrity, the Paris flight also made him wealthy. Although he refused many lucrative opportunities that were presented to him after the flight—a motion picture, vaudeville and lecture tours, advertising endorsements—he accepted others. Within two years the former airmail pilot who had had no particular prospects and only $2,000 to his name had accumulated a fortune of some $400,000.

He now moved among rich and powerful men. He quickly discovered that only such people could protect him from the crowds that dogged his every step and give him the privacy he desperately wanted. He wrote *We* in the seclusion of millionaire Harry Guggenheim's Long Island estate. On his frequent travels, he was grateful for the hospitality of rich men, since hotels proved intolerable. He married into the family—and thus the social circle—of a millionaire investment banker. Such men represented the very financial interests that Lindbergh's father had fought against all his life. But Lindbergh admired their mastery of great affairs and found their views congenial.

Charles and Anne Lindbergh with the Sirius, *the plane they flew to China in 1931 and to Europe and Africa in 1933.*
(Smithsonian Institution Photo No. A48532-L)

Not insincerely, Lindbergh became a public spokesman for the interests of his friends and employers. His family had always been Republican, so it was not unexpected that Lindbergh would vote for Herbert Hoover for president in 1928. But he also issued a public endorsement of Hoover—perhaps a presumptuous act for a 26-year-old aviator, though satisfying to his friends. The election of Democrat Franklin D. Roosevelt in 1932 ended business domination of the government. Not only were Lindbergh and his friends hostile to Roosevelt's New Deal, but Lindbergh found Roosevelt himself—jovial, gregarious, devious—personally distasteful.

Lindbergh emerged as a major anti-Roosevelt spokesman in 1934. A Senate investigation committee had discovered that preceding Republican administrations, following the transfer of airmail service from government to private hands, had awarded airmail contracts not to the lowest bidders as the law required but to certain favored airlines owned by major Wall Street interests. In February 1934 Roosevelt abruptly canceled those airmail contracts and ordered the army to carry the mail. But army pilots were unfamiliar with the airmail routes and untrained for night flying. In addition, the weather that February was unusually bad. In the first week of carrying the mail, five army pilots were killed, six were critically injured, and eight planes were wrecked. Lindbergh publicly attacked the administration and testified before a congressional committee on behalf of the airlines. The airmail service was soon returned to the airlines, though at reduced rates. Lindbergh's prestige and the army's failure had inflicted its first defeat on the new Roosevelt administration.

Lindbergh's distress over the constant invasion of his privacy became unbearable in February 1932 when his 20-month-old son, Charles Jr., was kidnapped from the Lindberghs' Hopewell, New Jersey, home. After a ransom was paid, the baby's body was found, not far from the house. In September 1934, Bruno Richard Hauptmann, a German immigrant working as a carpenter in the Bronx, was arrested for the crime. In January and February 1935 Hauptmann was tried and convicted, and in April 1936 he was executed. The Lindbergh kidnapping became "the crime of the century." Throughout the Lindberghs' long ordeal, the tabloid press was in a frenzy, exploiting each new development in the case to the fullest. When photographers turned their attention to the Lindberghs' second son, born in 1932, the Lindberghs decided they could find safety and privacy only outside the United States. In December 1935 they moved to England.

From 1936 to 1939, the Lindberghs lived in England and, later, France. At the invitation of the various governments, Charles was able to inspect the air forces of England, France, the Soviet Union, and Germany. He visited Germany half a dozen times, and Luftwaffe officials proudly displayed for him their factories, airfields, and newest military aircraft. It was clear to Lindbergh that Germany was building an air force technically and numerically superior to those of the other powers. Although he counseled the British and French to build up their air forces as rapidly as possible, the actual effect of his advice was to strengthen the advocates of defeatism and appeasement. Nothing could have been more satisfactory to the Germans. In October 1938, at a dinner party at the American embassy in Berlin, Luftwaffe chief Hermann Goering unexpectedly presented Lindbergh with a German decoration, ostensibly for his 1927 transatlantic flight. To many Americans, Lindbergh's acceptance, and especially his retention, of the decoration suggested a strange naïveté about the nature of the Nazi regime, if not actual sympathy for it.

The Lindberghs returned to the United States in April 1939. After war began in Europe in September, Lindbergh made a number of radio talks advocating a buildup of U.S. defenses but strict neutrality abroad. Later he became a leading spokesman for the America First Committee, an organization of influential isolationists. Lindbergh believed that England and France were decadent, and that Germany was invincible. In any case, the war was merely a continuation of an old struggle for leadership in Europe. The real conflict, he believed, was the one between the civilized West and barbaric Asia, as represented by Japan and especially by the Soviet Union. He envisioned a postwar Europe led by Nazi Germany and a Western Hemisphere led by the United States, together defending Western civilization against Asiatic hordes.

Lindbergh proved to be the most effective opponent of President Roosevelt's foreign policy. Roosevelt did not regard Nazi Germany as an exemplar of Western civilization. Moreover, he believed that Great Britain, with its navy, was necessary to the security of the United States, since the U.S. Navy was concentrated in the Pacific. He struggled against an isolationist Congress to provide Britain— which, after the fall of France in June 1940, stood alone against Germany—with all aid short of war. Recognizing Lindbergh's threat to his policy, Roosevelt, in an April 1941 press conference, compared Lindbergh to the Copperheads of the Civil War period, northerners who had sympathized with the South and had been defeatist about the Union cause. Believing that his loyalty had been impugned (as his father's had been during World War I), Lindbergh resigned his reserve commission.

In December 1941 Japan attacked Pearl Harbor, and shortly thereafter Germany declared war on the United States. Isolationism died. When Lindbergh sought reinstatement in the Army Air Corps, he was rebuffed. When he tried to find work in the aviation industry, the administration quietly prevented it. Eventually the automobile manufacturer Henry Ford, a former member of America First, hired Lindbergh as a consultant at his huge Willow Run plant, where the mass production of B-24 Liberator bombers was shortly to begin. Lindbergh improved the design of the plane, helped solve production problems and flight-tested the finished product. For the Republic Aircraft Corporation he conducted high-altitude tests of its P-47 Thunderbolt fighter. Then he became a consultant with the United Aircraft Corporation, trouble-shooting and testing its new F-4U Corsair, a navy and marine fighter and dive bomber.

In May 1944, without the knowledge of the administration in Washington, Lindbergh went to the South Pacific as a technical representative for United Aircraft to study the Corsair in action. His observer status permitted him to fly but not to fight. Nevertheless, with the complicity of local commanders, he did indeed fight, although he was a civilian and 42 years old. In marine Corsairs and army P-38 Lightnings, he flew strafing, dive-bombing, and pursuit missions. On July 28 he shot down a Japanese plane in a head-on duel.

More important than his combat flying, however, was Lindbergh's demonstration that the Corsair could carry twice the weight of bombs—4,000 pounds—that it was rated for and that the combat radius of the P-38 could be extended some 200 miles by using a lower throttle setting and a leaner fuel mixture during cruising.

Lindbergh was probably happier in the Pacific than he had been in 15 years. Politics was behind him. He was among men whose good opinion he valued. And he was doing something for which he had been trained and which he did superbly—flying fighters.

In September 1944, having flown 179 combat hours and 50 missions, Lindbergh returned quietly to the United States, his exploits in the Pacific only rumors.

Charles A. Lindbergh

After the war, Lindbergh went to Germany with a U.S. Naval Technical Mission to study German developments in aviation and rockets. He returned to Germany again in 1949 as an adviser to the U.S. Air Force during the Berlin airlift. In 1954, President Dwight D. Eisenhower restored his reserve commission and promoted him to brigadier general. He was appointed to the Air Force Scientific Advisory Board, in which capacity he tested new air force jets, flew patrols in the new B-52 bomber, and consulted on the U.S. manned space program. Pan American Airways elected him to its board of directors. In 1953 he published *The Spirit of St. Louis*, an expansion of the autobiography that he had first published as *We*. The book won the 1954 Pulitzer Prize for biography.

In his later years, Lindbergh became concerned that the progress of science and technology was increasingly divorcing people from other qualities of life and spirit, from nature itself. He became an active member of the World Wild Life Fund and other conservation organizations, working to save endangered species all over the world.

On August 26, 1974, Lindbergh died of lymphatic cancer at his home on the island of Maui in Hawaii.

The 1927 flight to Paris, when he was only 25 years old, was the central event of Lindbergh's life. Before the flight, he was an unknown barnstormer and mail pilot; after it, he was a celebrity of a magnitude unprecedented in American history. Historians and social scientists have tried in vain to fathom the delirium of adulation that surrounded the boyish aviator in 1927 and that never entirely vanished.

To a large extent the Paris flight was a stunt—a feat that looked more dangerous than it was. As he had done in his earlier escapades, Lindbergh had carefully calculated the odds and had found them in his favor. He and other aviators knew perfectly well that, with the appearance of the new air-cooled radial Wright Whirlwind engine, a flight to Paris was for the first time quite feasible. Only 10 years before, the wartime Liberty engines had been tested to ensure 50 hours of operation before breakdown; in factory tests, the Wright Whirlwind averaged 9,000 hours. A plane equipped with such an engine and capable of carrying sufficient fuel—and the *Spirit of St. Louis* carried virtually nothing but fuel—could hardly fail to make a 40-hour flight from New York to Paris. The only elements of risk that Lindbergh could not avoid were weather and sleeplessness. He was lucky with the weather. That he was able to stay awake, after a sleepless night before the flight, was a tribute to his iron self-discipline.

Stunt or not, Lindbergh's flight was central to the history of American aviation. More than any other single event, it made America air-minded. Lindbergh's celebrity shed luster on aviation itself. Immediately after the Paris flight, dozens of aviators, with all kinds of motives, undertook to establish new records in speed, altitude and endurance. "First flights" between distant places regularly made headlines. The business of the fledgling airlines expanded rapidly—the number of airline passengers grew from fewer than 6,000 in 1926 to more than 173,000 in 1929. Suddenly financing became available, not only for record-seeking fliers but also for constructive investment in technological development and industrial organization.

More than a few observers of Lindbergh's flight were inspired by its imagined significance for international relations. The Wright brothers had anticipated that the airplane would bring nations closer together, and indeed Lindbergh's flight markedly improved Franco-American relations. Ambassador Dwight Morrow recognized this positive effect and quickly drafted Lindbergh to make a goodwill flight to Latin America; for a time this helped to decrease popular hostility there toward the United States.

As for Lindbergh himself, in the heroic days of aviation he epitomized the aviator as hero. As flier, technician, and scientist he manifested true genius. Unfortunately, his prominence in aviation led him into politics, where his personal prejudices, lack of understanding of people, and ignorance of history colored his judgment. The controversy that even today surrounds his name obscures his many contributions to aviation—the improvement of aircraft, the pioneering of new air routes, the repeated testing of the limits of the possible.

Chronology

February 4, 1902	born in Detroit, Michigan
1918	graduates from high school in Little Falls, Minnesota, works on family farm

Charles A. Lindbergh

1920   enters the University of Wisconsin but drops out in his sophomore year

1922   enrolls in a flying school in Lincoln, Nebraska, begins career as stuntman and barnstormer

1923   soloes for first time

1924   enlists in U.S. Army, trains at Brooks and Kelly Fields, San Antonio, Texas

1925   commissioned second lieutenant, resigns from Army, resumes barnstorming

1926   becomes mail pilot for Robertson Aviation Company in St. Louis

1927   flies New York–Paris nonstop, tours U.S. cities, makes goodwill flight to Latin America

1929   marries Anne Morrow, becomes consultant with Pan American Airways

1931   surveys Arctic route to China

1932   infant son kidnapped and murdered in "crime of the century"

1933   surveys North Atlantic route to Europe, continues on to Africa and South America

1936   lives in England, then France, studies air forces of European powers

1939   returns to United States, speaks out against U.S. intervention in the war in Europe

1941   a leading spokesman for the America First Committee, he resigns his Army commission when President Roosevelt criticizes him

1942   works as a consultant to several airplane manufacturers

1944	makes inspection tour of the South Pacific, flies 50 combat missions although a civilian
1954	restored to Air Force with rank of brigadier general
August 26, 1974	dies in Maui, Hawaii

Further Reading

Books by Charles A. Lindbergh

We. New York: Putnam's, 1927. A short autobiography and account of his Paris flight, written immediately afterward. A best-seller when published, it has remained popular with young readers.

The Spirit of St. Louis. New York: Scribner's, 1953. An expansion of his earlier autobiography and record of his flight to Paris, this volume won a Pulitzer Prize.

Adult Biographies

Davis, Kenneth S. *The Hero: Charles A. Lindbergh and the American Dream*. Garden City, N.Y.: Doubleday, 1959. The first major biography of Lindbergh and still the best, although written while Lindbergh was still alive.

Gill, Brendan. *Lindbergh Alone*. New York: Harcourt Brace Jovanovich, 1977. A short, impressionistic biography reflecting on the forces that shaped Lindbergh's character.

Young-Adult Books

Lindbergh, Anne Morrow. *Listen! The Wind*. New York: Harcourt Brace, 1938. An eloquent description of one portion of the survey flight to Europe and Africa in 1933 by Lindbergh's wife and copilot.

Lindbergh, Anne Morrow. *North to the Orient*. New York: Harcourt Brace, 1935. Mrs. Lindbergh's charming and exciting account of the flight to China in 1931.

Randolph, Blythe. *Charles Lindbergh*. New York: Franklin Watts, 1990. A short, objective biography with many black-and-white photographs.

Bernt Balchen

Bernt Balchen in 1933.
(Smithsonian Institution Photo No. 91-8245)

On Thursday morning, May 19, 1927, 28-year-old Bernt Balchen caught a train in Garden City and went into New York, where he took out his first American citizenship papers. He was back at Roosevelt Field, Long Island, late that afternoon. That night, as he had done for several nights now, he slept on a cot in the hangar where Commander Richard E. Byrd's big trimotor Fokker monoplane was being prepared for its transatlantic flight. All night the rain drummed on the hangar roof. At one point Balchen heard a truck grind by, towing an airplane toward the runway. Later an automobile sped by. At dawn, Tony Fokker, his employer, burst into the hangar. "Quick!" he exclaimed. "Get some fire extinguishers. That young fool is going to take off."

Balchen and Fokker rushed out into the dripping dawn. At the end of the runway sat the little silver monoplane the *Spirit of St. Louis*, its engine idling. In a few minutes, its tall, lean pilot arrived. It was Charles Lindbergh, the airmail pilot from St. Louis of whom no one had heard a week before. Lindbergh examined the plane closely, studied the glistening runway for a while, and then climbed aboard. The engine roared, coughed. At 7:52 the over-loaded plane started down the runway, splashing through pud-dles, gaining speed slowly. At the very end of the runway its wheels finally left the ground. The little plane dipped into a depression beyond the runway, then rose and climbed away into the morning mist. Balchen murmured, *"Lykke paa reisen!"* (Luck on the voyage!)

Balchen—born in Tveit, Norway, on October 23, 1899—was a lieutenant in the Royal Norwegian Naval Air Force. In 1926 he had accompanied Norwegian explorer Roald Amundsen to Spitsbergen to help him prepare for his flight in the dirigible *Norge* across the North Pole to Alaska. Also in Spitsbergen that spring was a short, slender, unfailingly polite but tightly reserved U.S. naval officer, Lieutenant Commander Richard E. Byrd, who was determined to reach the pole first in his Fokker trimotor, the *Josephine Ford*. Byrd was to be the navigator on the flight. His pilot was a lanky, likable navy aviation mechanic named Floyd Bennett. For some reason, it proved impossible for the Fokker to take off from its packed-snow runway. Balchen, who had consid-erable experience with ski-equipped planes, volunteered advice that solved the problem.

On May 9, 1926, Byrd and Bennett succeeded in getting the *Josephine Ford* off the snow. They flew to the North Pole and returned, a distance of 1,360 miles, in less than 16 hours. Two days later Amundsen and his American partner, Lincoln Ellsworth, left Spitsbergen in the *Norge*, piloted by its Italian builder, Umberto Nobile, crossed the pole, and reached Alaska on May 14.

Following his triumph, Byrd invited Balchen to return to the United States with him and take part in a proposed Antarctic expedition. Balchen accompanied Byrd to America, flew the *Jose-phine Ford* on a two-month, 50-city exhibition tour with Bennett, and then—because Byrd had postponed his Antarctic venture—went to work as a test pilot for the famous Dutch airplane designer Anthony Fokker, at his factory in Hasbrouck Heights, New Jersey.

Byrd postponed his Antarctic expedition because he had be-come intrigued by the challenge of a transatlantic flight. For seven years, the Orteig prize—$25,000 for the first nonstop flight be-tween New York and Paris—had gone unclaimed. But airplanes were now capable of making the 3,600-mile flight, and pilots in the United States and Europe were preparing for it.

Bernt Balchen

The idea of a first transatlantic flight between major cities—Alcock and Brown had flown 1,700 miles from Newfoundland to Ireland in 1919—must have appealed to Byrd, who was intensely competitive and ambitious. Publicly, he professed to disdain the whole idea of a prize competition. It was certainly possible, he believed, for a stripped-down, single-engine plane loaded with gasoline to make the trip. But that would be only a stunt, contributing nothing to the progress of aviation. Byrd saw the excitement over a transatlantic flight as an opportunity to demonstrate the feasibility of safe, reliable international commercial aviation. He would make the flight in a multiengine craft, equipped with every navigational, communications, and safety device, and large enough to carry not only a crew but cargo or passengers as well. But first, money had to be raised, an airplane built, equipment procured, tests conducted, and government cooperation obtained. Fortunately for Byrd, a millionaire aviation enthusiast, Rodman Wanamaker, was prepared to finance the entire venture. His only requirements were that the airplane be called the *America* and that all its crew be U.S. citizens.

To build the *America*, Byrd in January 1927 went to Tony Fokker, who had built the *Josephine Ford*. Fokker was pioneering the use of tubular steel structure and plywood-sheathed wings, creating an airframe so strong that it would require a minimum of guy wires and struts. Byrd ordered a trimotor ship like the *Josephine Ford*, but capable of lifting 15,000 pounds and flying 4,000 miles. Fokker designed a plane to Byrd's specifications. Its 71-foot wingspan was eight feet longer than that of the *Josephine Ford*. In addition to fuel tanks in its wings, there was a large tank in the fuselage behind the pilot's cabin. A dump valve, devised by Byrd, permitted the pilot to jettison all his fuel in case of an imminent crash or a ditching at sea. In the latter case, the empty tanks would keep the plane floating indefinitely. The plane also had a switch, invented by Floyd Bennett, that could cut off all three engines simultaneously in a crash.

The *America* was tested for the first time on April 20 at Fokker's New Jersey factory. Fokker flew it himself, but Byrd insisted on going along and bringing Floyd Bennett, his pilot for the transatlantic flight, and George Noville, his radio operator. The plane performed as expected until Fokker attempted to land. Only then did he discover that with the fuselage fuel tank empty and all four men crowded into the cockpit, the plane was fatally nose-heavy. The plane crashed and overturned. Bennett's switch prevented a fire, but Byrd broke his arm, Noville suffered torn stomach muscles and Bennett received multiple, life-threatening injuries. Only Fokker escaped unhurt.

The plane had to be rebuilt. To better distribute the crew's weight, Fokker located the station for the navigator—Byrd—behind the fuselage fuel tank. To communicate with the cockpit, the navigator would have to drag himself on his belly along a catwalk beneath the tank. On May 13, Bernt Balchen tested the rebuilt ship briefly, then flew it from New Jersey to Roosevelt Field on Long Island, which Wanamaker had leased for Byrd's exclusive use. Many more tests remained to be performed, since the custom-built plane was an unknown quantity. Balchen stayed at Roosevelt Field, sleeping on a cot in the *America's* hangar.

By now the New York–Paris race had become a national sensation. Three planes had already been lost and six men killed in preparing for or attempting the flight. When Balchen brought the *America* into Roosevelt Field, he could see the single- engine planes of two other contenders already poised on adjacent Curtiss Field—Clarence Chamberlin's *Columbia* and Lindbergh's *Spirit of St. Louis*.

Still, Byrd refused to admit he was in a race—perhaps because he had just lost a valuable month and was far from ready to take off. In fact, he had not formally registered as a contestant for the Orteig prize. He was determined to test his plane thoroughly and equip it with care. To show the world that he was not competing with Chamberlin and Lindbergh, he invited the other pilots to use Roosevelt Field, whose runway had been extended especially for him. They also shared the weather information that Byrd had arranged for the U.S. Weather Bureau to assemble from data collected by the Radio Corporation of America from ships in the Atlantic. But the public refused to accept Byrd's disclaimers, and his own crew itched to be off.

His crew was a major problem for Byrd. The injured Floyd Bennett was unable to make the flight. In his place, Byrd hired Bert Acosta, considered the most gifted natural pilot in America and a well-known aerial daredevil whose specialties included flying upside down at low altitudes and picking up a handkerchief from the ground with a wing tip. But it turned out that Acosta knew nothing about instrument flying. At night or in bad weather, he was helpless. A copilot experienced in instrument flying was needed. Bernt Balchen, who had taken out his citizenship papers for just such an eventuality, was selected.

Lindbergh took off early Friday morning, May 20. The next afternoon, a thousand invited guests gathered at Roosevelt Field for the christening of the *America*. The ceremonies were interrupted by the news of Lindbergh's safe arrival in Paris. Betraying no sign of disappointment, Byrd paid gracious tribute to Lindbergh's skill and courage.

Chamberlin took off on June 4 with the *Columbia*'s owner as copilot. Since Lindbergh had already won the Orteig prize by flying to Paris, Chamberlin headed for Berlin. His plane was forced down at Eisleben, Germany, 100 miles short of Berlin but 300 miles farther than Lindbergh had flown.

Neither of these flights had accomplished what Byrd aimed to do—demonstrate the practicality of transatlantic commercial aviation. He continued his meticulous preparations for the flight of the *America*. Balchen and Acosta tested the plane for speed, rate of climb, and fuel consumption at various speeds and loads. Byrd, meanwhile, stockpiled 800 pounds of navigation and survival equipment. There were, of course, the navigation instruments that Byrd himself would use. There were also a wireless radio set, two inflatable rubber boats, a waterproof radio with kite antenna, a three-week food supply, a water-distilling apparatus and a medical kit. When all was finally ready, the weather proved unfavorable. Not until June 29 did Byrd give the order to depart.

Rain was falling lightly at 3:30 A.M. when the crew boarded the *America*. Acosta sat in the pilot's seat, Noville beside him where he could operate the radio and the fuel dump valve. Byrd and Balchen climbed through the afterhatch into the navigator's compartment located behind the fuel tank in the center of the fuselage. The *America* had been pulled up onto a 15-foot-high incline, its tailskid held by a rope. The idea—it was Fokker's—was to build up the engines to maximum revolutions per minute, at which point a ground crewman would cut the rope with an ax, causing the plane to hurtle down the incline and along the runway at full speed. The effect would be the equivalent of an additional 500 to 700 feet of runway. At 5:20 Acosta started the engines, but before they were fully warmed up the rope snapped and the plane lurched forward. Holding the plane onto the runway, Acosta shoved the throttle forward. The plane lumbered down the mile-long runway, laboring to gain speed. At the end of the runway Acosta pulled it into the air. The big plane climbed slowly through the morning mist. They were off.

Richard E. Byrd's America, *with Bert Acosta at the controls, taking off for Paris from Roosevelt Field, Long Island, June 29, 1927.*
(Smithsonian Institution Photo No. 91-8246)

The great circle route led over the eastern end of Long Island, across Cape Cod, over Nova Scotia and Newfoundland. Beyond Long Island, the sky cleared. They flew at 2,000 feet, the altitude of optimum fuel efficiency for the *America*. Over Nova Scotia, clouds gathered, and they climbed to 5,000 feet. By the time they reached St. John's, Newfoundland, the earth's surface was hidden by fog and cloud. For the next 2,000 miles they flew by instruments.

Night fell as they left Newfoundland behind. Their air-speed indicator registered 90 miles per hour, but tail winds added 30 more. Byrd frequently dragged himself under the main fuel tank to the cockpit to communicate with Acosta and Noville. Communication was by written notes; the roar of the three engines made speech impossible. Noville tapped out on the wireless progress reports composed by Byrd. Balchen also came forward to the cockpit, taking Noville's seat and spelling Acosta at the controls.

During the night Noville reported that fuel consumption was unexpectedly high; they might not have enough to reach Europe. Balchen and Acosta, who had tested the plane thoroughly, were perplexed. For a moment the fliers considered turning back, but they decided to go on. There had indeed been a leak in the main fuel tank, which Byrd had repaired with putty—but that was not the problem. Fokker had overcompensated for the former nose-heaviness of the ship, with the result that the tail was riding low and gasoline was not flowing to the gauges. But as the load lightened, the tail rose and the gauges read correctly. There was plenty of fuel.

At one point during the night, while Acosta had the controls, Balchen, who was sitting beside him, suddenly felt the plane go out of control into a spiraling dive. Air speed climbed to 140 miles per hour. At 160 the wing would come off. Balchen seized the controls and gently brought the plane out of its dive and back on course. Acosta, a traditional "seat of the pants" pilot, had paid no attention to the instruments, trusting to his instincts. In clouds and darkness, with no horizon below and no stars above, his instincts proved deceitful.

Morning came with no break in the clouds. In the afternoon of June 30 the clouds at last began to break up and they saw the surface of the ocean. At 5 P.M. they crossed the French coast at Brest, south of their intended course. Instead of following the Brest-Paris railroad to the capital, Byrd ordered the plane northeast along the coast to Le Havre, from where he would follow the River Seine.

They reached Le Havre at dusk. But now clouds had regathered and rain fell. From the wireless, they learned that the weather at Paris was bad—low clouds, heavy rain, no visibility. Balchen had the controls now. To follow the river he descended as low as 200 feet, but the clouds dropped even lower. He climbed to 4,000 feet and flew by instruments. When he calculated that he was over Paris, he descended, but could find no hole in the clouds and could see nothing on the ground. He turned back to Le Havre, then headed for Paris again, still on instruments. At 1 A.M. on July 1 they were over Paris again but still could see nothing. Now fuel was running out.

Byrd ordered them back to the coast, but they could find no place to land. It would be necessary to ditch the *America* at sea, close to shore. Byrd dropped flares onto the ocean surface, and Balchen brought the *America* down in shallow water. The plane's nose sank and touched bottom. Water poured in, but the crew escaped and clambered up onto the wing, which, like the fuselage, was buoyed up by empty fuel tanks. From the emergency hatch they extracted a rubber boat, inflated it, and paddled 200 yards to shore. At 4:40 A.M., on July 1, 1927, the Byrd transatlantic expedition arrived in France.

The celebrations that greeted Byrd and his crew in Paris and New York—only slightly less exuberant than those that had greeted Lindbergh—had barely faded when Byrd began planning his postponed Antarctic expedition. Amundsen had reached the South Pole by dogsled in December 1911, and Robert F. Scott 35 days later, in January 1912. Byrd made the obvious point that with airplanes, cameras, and radio he could cover more ground in an hour than land-bound explorers could in a week. But his real motive was simply to be the first man to fly over both the North and South Poles. And, as usual, time was of the essence. Other explorers—the Australians Sir George Wilkins and Sir Douglas Mawson, and a Norwegian, Hjalmar Riiser-Larsen—were preparing polar flights.

The Byrd Antarctic expedition established its base, Little America, on the Ross Ice Shelf at the Bay of Whales—near Amundsen's 1911 camp—in January 1929. The site was the closest approach by sea to the pole, which lay 850 miles away across the Ross Ice Shelf, the Queen Maud Mountains, and the high polar plateau. The expedition included three airplanes. There was a small, single-engine Fairchild, a larger single-engine Fokker, and a Ford trimotor named the *Floyd Bennett* after Byrd's companion on previous expeditions, who had died in 1928. The trimotor was equipped with a new 525-horsepower Wright Cyclone engine in its nose and two 220-horsepower Wright Whirlwinds on its wings. Fully loaded, it weighed 15,000 pounds and had a top speed of 122 miles per hour. Its ceiling, however, was considerably below the 14,000-foot peaks of the Queen Maud range. This was the plane with which Byrd hoped to reach the pole. The Fokker was his long-range rescue plane, and the Fairchild was for local flying. Bernt Balchen was the expedition's chief aviator.

As soon as their base was established, Balchen flew Byrd in the Fairchild on a short exploratory flight 100 miles east of Little America, where Byrd sighted a hitherto unknown mountain range that he named the Rockefeller Mountains after one of the expedition's benefactors. In March, Balchen flew the expedition's geologist to the mountains in the Fokker. While the plane was on the ground, gale force winds wrecked it. The geological party was rescued by Byrd in the Fairchild. Relieved that his men had not been killed, Byrd was concerned that he now had no long-range rescue plane. If the Ford trimotor went down on the polar plateau, there would be no way to save its crew.

The Fairchild and the Ford spent the Antarctic winter in hangars excavated from the ice and walled with snow blocks over which tarpaulins were spread. These immediately froze solid and were soon covered with snow. When the sun returned in September, plans for the polar flight were put into high gear.

Early in November 1929, a geological party set off by dogsled on a three-month, 450-mile journey of exploration to the Queen Maud range. Its primary mission, however, was not exploration but the establishment of supply depots along the line that the Ford trimotor would take on its way to and from the pole. The explorers were also to act as a rescue party in case the *Floyd Bennett* came down on the Ross Ice Shelf.

Meanwhile, the Fairchild and the Ford were exhumed from their snow hangars, tuned up, and test flown. On November 18, Byrd, with pilot Dean Smith, copilot Harold June, and photographer Ashley McKinley, flew in the Ford to the Queen Maud range to establish a supply depot at its base. On the way back to Little America, the Ford ran out of fuel and came down on the snow, its radio also inoperative. Back at Little America, Balchen deduced what had happened to the overdue plane. Carrying 100 gallons of gasoline in five-gallon cans, he flew the Fairchild along the Ford's route and found the trimotor 100 miles out. He left the gasoline and returned to base. But again the Ford failed to arrive. Balchen returned to the stranded plane to discover that Smith and June had been unable to restart the frozen engines. Balchen started them, and at last the two planes returned safely to Little America.

More than ever, Byrd realized how fragile these planes were in the Antarctic cold and how fortunate he had been that both planes had now made several emergency landings on the snow without damage. Luck like that could not be expected to hold. If he had been uncertain before, he now decided that Balchen would pilot the polar flight.

On November 27 the geological party radioed that the weather near the Queen Maud range was ideal. Byrd decided that the polar flight would take place the next day, Thanksgiving Day. The *Floyd Bennett* was already thoroughly checked and loaded with 1,400 pounds of emergency gear. That afternoon Balchen took the pilot's seat, Harold June the copilot and radio operator's seat. Ashley McKinley stationed himself at the bottom hatch with his mapping camera. Byrd took the navigator's station back in the fuselage, from where he communicated with the cockpit by means of a trolley cable. At 3:29 P.M. on November 28, Balchen flipped

*Bernt Balchen (left) and Floyd Bennett with the single-engine Fokker that
Richard Byrd took to the Antarctic in 1929.*
(Smithsonian Institution Photo No. A4136-C)

the plane's rudder to loosen the skis, gunned the motors, and took
off into an 18-mile-per-hour easterly wind.

The Ford climbed to 1,500 feet and turned directly south,
picking up the trail that the geological party had made three weeks
before. The route was virtually the same that Amundsen had
followed in 1911. Flying at 90 miles per hour, the *Floyd Bennett*
overtook the geological party in under four hours. At 8:50 the
Queen Maud range loomed ahead, its peaks lost in the clouds. Two

glaciers, flowing between sheer, towering cliffs, cut passes through the mountains. Amundsen had reported that the highest point of the Axel Heiberg Glacier was 10,500 feet, but today its summit was hidden in clouds. The fliers turned west to Liv's Glacier. Its summit, which they estimated to be 9,500 feet, was clear. Balchen guided the Ford between the cliffs and followed the cataract of ice upward. As they proceeded, the canyon narrowed. Soon there was no room to turn around. At 8,200 feet the heavily loaded Ford could go no higher. June dumped a 150-pound bag of emergency rations and the plane lifted higher.

"A final icy wall blocks our way, steeper than all the others," Balchen related of this flight. "A torrent of air is pouring over its top, the plane bucking violently in the downdraft, and our rate of climb is zero. June jettisons the second sack, and the Ford staggers a little higher, but still not enough. There is only one thing left to try. Perhaps at the very edge of the downdraft is a reverse current of air, like a back-eddy along the bank of a rushing river, that will carry us upstream and over. I inch my way to the side of the canyon, our right wing almost scraping the cliff, and all at once we are wrenched upward, shooting out of the maelstrom of winds, and soar over the summit with a couple of hundred feet to spare."

Now they were over the polar plateau, a flat empty expanse of snow. Somewhere in that dazzling white plain, 400 miles away, was the South Pole. Balchen set his course along the 171st meridian and flew south at 11,000 feet. The mountains faded behind them. Ahead of them was an empty horizon. At 1:14 A.M. on November 29, 1929, Byrd sent a penciled note forward on the trolley for June to broadcast to Little America: "We have reached the South Pole." From Little America the report was immediately relayed to the outside world. Meanwhile Byrd directed Balchen to fly back and forth across the area. At the point he calculated was the pole, Byrd dropped an American flag weighted with a stone from Floyd Bennett's grave. Then the fliers turned and retraced their route, across the polar plateau, down Liv's Glacier through the Queen Maud Mountains, across the Ross Ice Shelf. At 10 A.M. the Ford landed at Little America.

Little America was dismantled in February 1930, and the explorers returned home to tumultous welcomes in New York and Washington. Byrd was promoted to rear admiral; there were medals for the expedition members; and for Balchen, Congress passed a special act granting him full U.S. citizenship.

Four years later Balchen was again in Antarctica, as chief pilot of the 1933–35 Ellsworth Antarctic expedition. During the years 1935 to 1940 he was back in Norway, where he helped organize Norwegian Airlines and served as its chief inspector, planning and flying new routes.

With the outbreak of World War II, Balchen joined Britain's RAF Ferry Command, flying American-built PBY flying boats from California to Hong Kong and Singapore. In 1941 he was commissioned a captain in the U.S. Army Air Force and assigned to build and command a base above the Arctic Circle on the west coast of Greenland for the use of military airplanes flying between the United States and England by way of Greenland and Iceland. His stay in Greenland was marked by dramatic rescues of American fliers downed on the ice and by the destruction of a German weather station on Greenland's east coast.

In 1944–45, Colonel Balchen commanded an operation of the U.S. Office of Strategic Services, flying bombers between Scotland and neutral Sweden, from where he evacuated 5,000 Norwegian and other anti-Nazi refugees as well as interned U.S. fliers. The operation also dropped supplies to the Norwegian resistance.

After the war, Balchen remained in Norway as managing director of Norwegian Airlines and helped organize Scandinavian Airlines (SAS). In 1948 he was recalled at his own request to active duty in the U.S. Air Force and assigned to command the 10th Rescue Squadron in Alaska. Balchen retired from the Air Force in 1956. He died in Mount Kisco, New York, on October 17, 1973, just days short of his 74th birthday.

For 30 years, Bernt Balchen was involved in some of the most dramatic episodes of aviation history, always as a hired pilot, never as the initiator of an enterprise. His fellow pilots regarded him as one of the best, and his frequent employment in hazardous undertakings supports that reputation. Balchen's lasting contribution to aviation was his pioneering of polar flying. The advantages of exploring the Arctic and Antarctic from the air were apparent as early as 1897, when Salomon Andrée launched his ill-fated balloon into the Arctic wastes. During the 1920s and 1930s, explorations of the Arctic and Antarctic by dirigible and airplane were pursued by private expeditions whose best-known leaders were Roald Amundsen, Lincoln Ellsworth, Richard Byrd, Hubert Wilkins, Umberto Nobile, Donald MacMillan, Douglas Mawson, and Finn Ronne. Three of these explorers—Amundsen, Byrd, and Ellsworth—chose Balchen to assist them. In World War

II, Balchen continued to fly in the Arctic for the U.S. Army Air Force. The war marked the end of private exploration of polar regions. Thereafter, national governments sponsored well-equipped but largely anonymous teams of scientists to conduct exploration and research in the polar regions. The day of heroic adventurers like Bernt Balchen was over.

Chronology

October 23, 1899	born in Tveit, Norway
1924	commissioned lieutenant in the Royal Norwegian Naval Air Force
1925	directs successful search for Arctic fliers Roald Amundsen and Lincoln Ellsworth
1926	accompanies Amundsen to Spitsbergen, meets Richard E. Byrd, goes to the United States
1927	copilot on Byrd's transatlantic flight, makes forced landing off French coast
1929	pilots Byrd from Little America to South Pole and back
1933	appointed chief pilot for Ellsworth Antarctic expedition
1935	employed by Norwegian Airlines
1940	ferries British flying boats from California to Far East
1941	joins U.S. Army Air Force, commands base in Greenland
1944	flies supplies to Norwegian resistance, rescues U.S. fliers interned in Sweden
1946	returns to Norwegian Airlines
1948	recalled to active duty in U.S. Air Force, commands 10th Rescue Squadron in Alaska

1956	retires from Air Force
October 17, 1973	dies in Mount Kisco, New York

Further Reading

Book by Bernt Balchen
Come North with Me. New York: Dutton, 1958. A delightful autobiography, crammed with fascinating, well-told adventure stories.

Amelia Earhart

*Amelia Earhart emerging from her Lockheed Vega after her
solo flight from Hawaii to California, January 12, 1935.*
(Albert Bresnick photo)

Kinner Field was a 50-acre expanse of dirt and weeds a mile from
the end of the electric streetcar line from Los Angeles. There Bert
Kinner had erected a wind sock and a tin-roofed hangar where
pilots could tinker with their planes while waiting for passengers
or students. Kinner himself worked on a small light biplane of his
own design, the Kinner Airster.

One day in December 1920, a tall, slender 23-year-old woman, well-dressed in a brown suit and gloves and accompanied by her father, arrived at the field and inquired for Anita Snook, the only female pilot among the handful of men who lounged about the hangar. "I'm Amelia Earhart," she told Anita Snook, "and this is my father. I want to learn to fly and I understand you teach students. Will you teach me?"

Short, red-haired, and vivacious, Anita Snook agreed. Only a year older than Amelia, she owned a two-seater Canuck, the Canadian version of the Curtiss Jenny that had been the U.S. Army trainer during World War I. The two young women became good friends. "Neta" Snook gave Amelia lessons in her Canuck and then in the Kinner Airster, which Amelia bought the next July using some of her own money and some borrowed from her mother and sister. A former army pilot gave her additional instruction. Amelia delayed soloing for more than six months. Although she was intelligent enough, she lacked the natural talent that distinguished good pilots from the merely competent. Carelessness and daydreaming frequently got her into trouble. But what she lacked in talent she made up for in enthusiasm.

Amelia Earhart was born on July 24, 1897, in Atchison, Kansas, the home of her mother's wealthy and prominent family. Amelia's father, a Kansas City lawyer, was only intermittently successful. Bad luck and alcohol dogged his steps, and the marriage eventually ended in divorce.

Despite their pretensions to social status, the Earharts were economically insecure. Amelia and her younger sister, Muriel, moved with their parents from Kansas City to Des Moines, then to St. Paul, then to Chicago as their father pursued a succession of disappointing jobs. Amelia attended six high schools, finally graduating in 1915 from Hyde Park High School in Chicago. For a time she attended a private college-preparatory school in Philadelphia, but she dropped out to become a nurse's aid in a Toronto military hospital during the last year of World War I.

After the war, Amelia enrolled in Columbia University in New York as a premed student, but she left after a semester to rejoin her family, now living in Los Angeles. There she worked at a variety of jobs, with no particular purpose or direction. Her discovery of aviation awoke her first serious enthusiasm. Thereafter, all her jobs served only to finance her flying lessons, the purchase of the Kinner Airster, and her infrequent flights. (Like the other pilots who hung out at Kinner Field, Amelia could fly only when she could afford to buy gasoline.) In October 1922 she took her parents to an air show in which, to their surprise, she participated, establishing a new women's altitude record of 14,000 feet in the Kinner Airster. The record stood for only a few weeks.

In 1923 the family suffered severe financial reverses. Amelia sold her airplane, her parents separated, and she and her mother moved to Boston. There in 1925 Amelia got a job at $35 a week as a social worker at Denison House, a settlement house, helping poor immigrants. She spent her spare time at local airfields, flying occasionally and garnering some local newspaper publicity as a female pilot. Then, one day in 1928, a telephone call to her at Denison House changed her life.

The caller represented George Palmer Putnam, a man of many talents and inexhaustible energy, of whom Amelia had never heard. Primarily, he was a book publisher, working in the family firm, G.P. Putnam's Sons in New York. But he was also an agent, publicist, and promoter, often for the authors and celebrities whose books he published. Celebrity was virtually invented in the 1920s. All sorts of people—movie stars, sports heroes, explorers, aviators—had their hour of fame (or notoriety) in the headlines of the nation's newspapers. Putnam realized that there was money to be made in the "fame business," not only for the celebrity but also for the celebrity's agent. Books, magazine articles, lectures, and advertising endorsements could earn substantial sums before the public's attention turned to some new sensation.

As a publisher, Putnam had discovered that adventure books sold. It was an obvious next step to help his adventurer authors to capitalize further on their celebrity. His company published the books of jungle explorers Marten and Osa Johnson and William Beebe, of Arctic explorers Knud Rasmussen and Robert Bartlett. In 1927 Putnam published *Skyward*, Richard Byrd's account of his first flight over the North Pole. The same year the company published *We*, Charles Lindbergh's story of his sensational transatlantic solo flight. George Putnam himself caught the adventure bug. In 1926 he organized an expedition to Greenland, and the following year he led one to Baffin Island in the Arctic Ocean. On both occasions he managed to make headlines in the *New York Times*, and on his return he added lecturing to his many other activities.

Always on the lookout for the next celebrity—preferably a "property" he could profitably manage—Putnam in 1928 heard that several women were preparing to attempt flights across the Atlantic Ocean. One wealthy aviation enthusiast had gone so far as to lease an airplane and hire a pilot and mechanic to ferry her across. At the last minute, her family persuaded her to abandon the attempt. Putnam realized that if he could find another woman to go in her place, he would have a celebrity of his own creation. The trick was to find the right woman. She had to be an aviator, of course, although she would be only a passenger on the flight. She also had to be young, attractive, well bred, and well educated—in short, she had to be a lady. Putnam heard that there was just such a person working as a social worker in Boston.

Speaking to Amelia on the telephone at Denison House, Putnam's representative told her only that he was organizing an exciting aviation venture; would she be interested? The next day, properly chaperoned by another female Denison House worker, Amelia appeared for an interview with the caller. He immediately asked: "How would you like to be the first woman to fly the Atlantic?"

There were other interviews, in Boston and New York, with Putnam and other organizers of the flight. Putnam was immediately impressed by the tall, slim, blue-eyed, tousled-haired, self-possessed young woman, who bore an uncanny resemblance, both in appearance and manner, to last year's hero, Charles Lindbergh. Putnam explained the details of the venture. The flight would be from Boston to Newfoundland and thence to London. The plane was a trimotor Fokker monoplane, each of whose engines generated 220 horsepower. It was equipped with aluminum pontoons for taking off and landing in water. Already named the *Friendship* to celebrate Anglo-American amity, it was even then being readied in Boston for the transatlantic flight.

Amelia had never been in so large a plane before. Nor had she had any experience with multiengine planes or with instrument flying. The plane would, in fact, be flown by an experienced pilot, Wilmer Stultz, and a copilot and flight mechanic, Lou Gordon. Amelia would be only a passenger, although nominally "commander" of the flight. She would receive no pay, but, Putnam pointed out, if the flight succeeded she could expect to make considerable money from personal appearances, articles, lectures, and, of course, a book that would be published by G. P. Putnam's Sons.

The prospect of financial reward was not a matter of indifference to Amelia, who was leading a penurious existence on her social worker's salary. But it was irrelevant to her prompt decision to accept the proposition. As she later said, "I thought all this out in the first five minutes and I knew I wanted to go. I went because

I love life and all it has to offer. I want every opportunity and adventure it can give."

On June 3, 1928, the *Friendship* lifted heavily off the water of Boston Harbor, bound for Trepassey Bay in Newfoundland. There bad weather delayed the ocean crossing for two weeks. Just before noon on June 17, the big plane took off from the rough surface of Trepassey Bay, its spray-soaked engines sputtering alarmingly. Once the engines achieved full power, the plane flew steadily, through fog, clouds, and darkness. At dawn, the crew hoped to sight Ireland, but they saw only open sea. Just after noon, with the fuel supply almost exhausted, they sighted land and put down in the sheltered bay off Burry Port, Wales.

Stultz, Gordon, and Earhart had no idea where they were, and the crowd that gathered on the shore did not know who the visitors were. But word soon spread. Reporters flew in from Southampton and London. The next morning the fliers were presented with a sackful of congratulatory telegrams, including one from the president of the United States, Calvin Coolidge—addressed to Amelia, the *Friendship*'s passenger.

That day the *Friendship* flew to Southampton, where the fliers were greeted by larger crowds and besieged by the press. From Southampton they traveled to London, where Amelia was greeted deliriously and swept up into a hectic round of activities celebrating the world's latest heroine. Although at every opportunity Amelia gave Stultz and Gordon full credit for the flight, the crowds were interested only in her. The two men faded gratefully into the background, while Amelia was interviewed by the world's press and feted by society.

Returning to New York by ship, the fliers were welcomed by more cheering throngs. There was the traditional ticker-tape parade up Broadway, and the mayor presented Amelia the key to the city. The next day the fliers traveled to Boston for another clamorous reception, then on to Chicago for yet another. After that, Stultz and Gordon disappeared. In the blizzard of publicity, only a few articles pointed out that Amelia had been only a passenger on the *Friendship*, that the flight had contributed nothing to aviation science, and that, in fact, the whole event had been a publicity stunt undertaken for profit.

Amelia did not return to her job at Denison House. She had a new career. There were countless offers for public appearances and speeches, for lectures and articles. She was appointed aviation editor of *Cosmopolitan* magazine. Her log of the flight was adapted for a book, *20 Hrs. 40 Min.*, published by Putnam's. She was now in the fame business, and George Putnam was her manager. Amelia was sincerely interested in promoting aviation and opportunities for women. Putnam was interested in promoting Amelia. His interest was personal as well as commercial; the two fell in love, and in 1931—after Putnam's divorce—they were married. If Amelia was not the best female pilot in America, he would make her the best known. The problem was to find continuously new exploits to keep Amelia in the public eye. The public's attention span was short. If one was going to make a living in the fame business, it was necessary that one's fame be regularly renewed.

In England after her transatlantic flight, anticipating the money she would earn on her return to the United States, Amelia bought an Avro Avian, a small two-seat open-cockpit biplane. Together with the *Friendship*, the Avian was crated and shipped to the United States. In September 1928 Amelia flew it from New York to California. There were many stops along the way and at least one accident, and at one point Amelia was completely lost. But she became the first woman to fly solo across the continent. The next month she flew back to New York. This trip was marked by a forced landing in which the Avian was damaged. But now Amelia had become the first woman to make a solo return transcontinental flight.

In 1929 Amelia and other women pilots organized a cross-country air race for women, the Los Angeles to Cleveland Women's Air Derby. Humorist Will Rogers dubbed it the Powder Puff Derby, and the name stuck. For the race, Amelia sold her small Avian and bought a powerful Lockheed Vega, a streamlined, closed-cabin monoplane with a 450-horsepower engine, fast but difficult to handle for a woman who was not particularly strong. Nineteen women started from Santa Monica, California, on August 18, 1929. Sixteen finished the race in Cleveland on August 26. Amelia came in third, two hours behind the winner. She had had an accident en route, and she made a dangerously poor landing in Cleveland. Friends who knew how difficult it was for her to control the powerful Vega admired her courage, if not her skill.

The next year, Amelia set a women's speed record of 181.18 miles per hour in the Vega. She also became interested in autogiros, a combination of airplane and modern helicopter. In April 1931 she set an altitude record for autogiros, and in May and June, using an autogiro owned by the Beech Nut chewing gum company, she flew from New York to California and back. The trip was marred by a serious accident in Texas, for which Amelia received an official reprimand for carelessness. In September, after demonstrating an autogiro at an air show in Detroit, she crashed on landing. The autogiro was destroyed, but Amelia walked away unhurt.

These and other activities received wide publicity. Putnam constantly planned new stunts, and publicized them with a flow of press releases heralding Amelia's achievements while suppressing information likely to detract from her growing reputation—such as the help she received from other pilots and the additional flight instruction she required to qualify for advanced licenses. Always the press releases explained Amelia's many mishaps as due to mechanical defects in the airplane or problems with the landing field, never to pilot error.

Still smarting from the criticisms of her 1928 transatlantic flight in which she had been only a passenger, Amelia had long thought about making a transatlantic solo flight. It was Putnam's inspiration to plan it for the fifth anniversary of Lindbergh's 1927 flight. This time, Amelia forestalled criticism by acknowledging that the flight had no scientific significance. "It was clear in my mind that I was undertaking the flight merely for the fun of it," she wrote. "It was, in a measure, a self-justification—a proving to me, and to anyone else interested, that a woman with adequate experience could do it."

Amelia left Teterboro Airport in New Jersey in her Lockheed Vega on May 20, 1932, five years to the day after Lindbergh's takeoff from Roosevelt Field on Long Island. On the first leg of the trip, to Harbour Grace, Newfoundland, the plane was flown by another pilot so as not to tire Amelia before the actual transocean flight. From Harbour Grace at sunset that same day, Amelia took off alone for London. Within a few hours her altimeter failed; a seam in the exhaust manifold split, causing the plane to vibrate; and a fuel leak developed. Meanwhile, she ran into a storm, ice, fog, and darkness. At dawn, over open sea and 200 miles off course, she resolved to put down at the first land she saw. At 1:45 P.M. on Saturday, May 21, she landed in a pasture near Londonderry in Northern Ireland.

Overnight, Amelia had established four new records. She was the first woman (and only the second person) to fly the Atlantic solo; she was the only person to have flown it twice; she had crossed in record time; and she had posted a new women's distance record.

From Ireland, Amelia was flown to London, where she was again acclaimed and celebrated as she had been in 1928. The Vega, having been shipped from Ireland, was put on public display. Then it was on to Paris, Rome, and Brussels for more frenzied receptions. Back in New York, there was another ticker-tape parade, dinner at the White House in Washington with President Herbert Hoover, and then a tour of other American cities. Before her flight, Amelia had completed the manuscript of a book in which she encouraged women to take up flying. In Europe she wrote a final chapter describing the transatlantic flight, and the finished book, *For the Fun of It* (1932), published at the height of her homecoming celebrations, became a best-seller.

The fame business permitted no rest. In August 1932 Amelia became the first woman to fly nonstop from coast to coast, establishing both a cross-country distance record and a women's speed record. In 1933 she broke her own speed record on another nonstop transcontinental flight. In January 1935, flying a new Vega, she became the first person to fly solo from Hawaii to California. Three months later, she became the first person to fly solo from Los Angeles to Mexico City and from Mexico City to Newark, New Jersey. All the while, she was constantly traveling, by plane and train, on the lecture circuit; writing and broadcasting; engaging in business ventures; and socializing with other celebrities—including President and Mrs. Franklin D. Roosevelt, whom Amelia and Putnam visited at the White House several times. In 1935 she accepted an appointment to the faculty of Purdue University in Lafayette, Indiana, where, for a few weeks each semester, she would lecture and advise on careers for women and consult with the university's aeronautics department. All these activities were widely reported by the press. It was no longer necessary for Putnam to beat the drums. Poll-takers found that the best-known women in America were Eleanor Roosevelt and Amelia Earhart.

What next? There were few attention-grabbing flights that had not yet been made. And the public was beginning to tire of aviation heroics. Thanks in part to the achievements of people like Amelia Earhart, aviation was rapidly developing from a sport for adventurers into a business for professionals. Moreover, the public's mood was growing serious, less susceptible to publicity stunts. In the United States, the Great Depression dragged grimly on. In Europe, war clouds gathered. There was already war in Asia.

84

Perhaps Amelia could make one last, dramatic flight—a flight around the world. The world had already been circumnavigated by air a number of times, most recently by the one-eyed pilot Wiley Post. In 1931, Post and a navigator flew around the world in less than nine days. Then in 1933, Post made the trip again, this time solo, in less than eight days. But no woman had yet made an around-the-world flight. Amelia would be the first, and she had the idea of doing it the long way—near the equator. Such a flight would have no scientific significance and it did not promise to be fun. But it was a challenge that Amelia felt impelled to accept. That was the sort of thing that being famous required.

An around-the-world flight in the 1930s was still extremely hazardous. For a start, it required a powerful airplane. Amelia selected a Lockheed Electra, whose two engines each produced 550 horsepower. Putnam had the brilliant idea that Purdue University should buy the plane, call it a "flying laboratory," and let Amelia use it, ostensibly to test the sophisticated new equipment that long-distance flights increasingly required. Purdue embraced the plan enthusiastically and raised a special fund to buy the plane. Amelia required lengthy instruction to handle the large ship, whose controls strained her modest strength.

Amelia's course would be westward from California. Putnam busied himself with planning the route and managing the logistics. Landing places had to be selected with care, permission to use them obtained from local governments, fuel and spare parts stockpiled in advance. Their friendship with the Roosevelts enabled Putnam and Amelia to obtain the cooperation of the U.S. government in such matters as charts, weather information, and communications for the long and dangerous Pacific leg of the journey.

Amelia took off from Oakland Airport for Hawaii on March 17, 1937. She was accompanied by three men—Paul Mantz, a pilot who had instructed her in flying the Electra; Fred Noonan, an expert navigator long employed by Pan American Airways; and Harry Manning, another navigator also expert in radio communications. Mantz was to go only as far as Hawaii; Noonan was to guide Amelia to her second stop, Howland Island, a tiny speck of land 1,800 miles southwest of Hawaii in the trackless Pacific; and Manning was to accompany her as far as Australia. With the Pacific crossing behind her, Amelia would then complete the round-the-world flight alone.

On the first leg of the flight, Mantz spelled Amelia at the controls of the Electra and made the landing at Honolulu. Already fatigued,

A crowd surrounds Amelia Earhart's plane at Oakland, California, after her Hawaii–California flight.
(Smithsonian Institution Photo No. 73-4032)

Amelia delayed starting the next leg for 24 hours. Then on March 20, while taking off, she lost control of the ship. Still on the ground, the speeding Electra spun around, its landing gear collapsed, and the plane was seriously damaged. Amelia emerged shaken but unhurt. She and Putnam attributed the accident, as usual, to mechanical failure.

The Electra was crated and returned to California, where it was extensively rebuilt. Amelia was determined to make another attempt, but since that would be later in the year when weather conditions would be different, the decision was made to reverse directions and fly east instead of west. Putnam had to remake all the costly logistical arrangements, while Mantz gave Amelia further instruction.

On May 29, 1937, Amelia took off from Los Angeles, bound for Miami. With her were Fred Noonan, Putnam, and another passenger. At Miami, a week was spent in final preparations. On June 1, Amelia and navigator Noonan took off again. By stages, Amelia flew the Electra to Natal in Brazil, across the Atlantic to Dakar in Senegal, across Africa to Eritrea, then across the Arabian Sea to Karachi (the first nonstop flight from Africa to India), and then on to Burma, Indonesia, Australia, and, on June 29, to Lae in Papua New Guinea. All along the route Amelia wrote brief articles about the flight that were cabled to the *New York Herald Tribune*. Later these were collected, edited, and published in book form as *Last Flight* (1937).

Lae was the jumping-off point for crossing the Pacific. The first stop would be tiny Howland Island, 2,556 miles away. Amelia and Noonan had been flying for a month. Amelia had been ill along the way and both were tired. They spent three days in Lae resting and preparing for the difficult Pacific crossing. On July 2 they took off again.

The flight from Lae to Howland Island should have taken about 18 hours. The U.S. Coast Guard cutter *Itasca* was stationed off Howland Island to provide radio contact with Amelia. It received its first transmission from her when the flight had been underway 14 hours and 15 minutes. Amelia's transmissions were irregular and varied in quality. Static made the first message unintelligible; later messages were too faint or incomplete to understand. After 18 hours, when the Electra should have been within sight of Howland Island, her transmission came in loud and clear. She was, she said, about 100 miles out. At no time did she acknowledge receipt of *Itasca*'s transmissions. At 19 hours 12 minutes into the flight, *Itasca* heard her broadcast: "We must be on you but cannot see you but gas is running low." A few minutes later Amelia and *Itasca* were in two-way contact for the first and only time. At 20 hours 14 minutes *Itasca* picked up its last message from Amelia. It was loud and clear but gave no useful indication of her position. After that, silence.

It was clear that the Electra was down in the Pacific. The *Itasca* steamed at once to the most likely area but found nothing. Over the next few weeks, a massive sea and air search was undertaken by the U.S. Navy involving nine ships and 66 airplanes. No trace of the Electra was found. The search was called off on July 18.

The extensive search for Amelia Earhart later gave rise to rumors that her flight and disappearance had been staged by the U.S. government to provide a cover for an aerial survey of the Marshall Islands. These former German possessions had been mandated after World War I to Japan, which was suspected of fortifying them illegally. No evidence has been found to support this or other stories suggesting that Amelia had been on a spy mission.

Amelia and Noonan probably died on July 3, 1937, when their plane ditched in the Pacific. The Electra could not float for more than a few minutes. Amelia was just three weeks short of her 40th birthday.

Amelia Earhart was a passionate flier whose enthusiasm and courage exceeded her abilities. In pursuit of fame, she felt compelled to take repeated and ever-greater risks in the sure knowledge that one day her luck would run out. Her fame enabled her to make a living in aviation, something that few less-celebrated aviators—male or female—could do. Aside from that, she used her fame for unselfish purposes—to improve international and especially Anglo-American relations, to make aviation familiar and acceptable to the public, and to widen opportunities for women in aviation and in other fields as well. In books, articles, and lectures she constantly advanced these causes, but never more effectively than by the example of her own remarkable achievements in the air.

Chronology

July 24, 1897	born in Atchison, Kansas
1918	serves as nurse in a military hospital in Toronto, Canada
1921	takes first flying lessons in Los Angeles
1922	sets unofficial women's altitude record
1925	becomes social worker at Denison House in Boston
1928	becomes first woman to fly the Atlantic (as passenger)
1929	takes third place in first Women's Air Derby from Santa Monica, California, to Cleveland, Ohio
1930	sets women's speed record
1931	sets autogiro altitude record, makes first transcontinental flight in autogiro

1932	flies the Atlantic from Newfoundland to Ireland
1933	sets transcontinental speed record
1935	becomes first person to fly solo from Honolulu, Hawaii to Oakland, California, then from Los Angeles to Mexico City; breaks speed record from Mexico City to Newark, New Jersey
1936	acquires twin-engine Lockheed Electra "Flying Laboratory"
1937	undertakes round-the-world flight
July 3, 1937	dies in the Pacific near Howland Island

Further Reading

Books by Amelia Earhart

The Fun of It: Random Records of My Own Flying and of Women in Aviation. New York: Brewer, Warran, & Putnam, 1932. Amelia reflects on her flying experiences and encourages women to get involved in aviation.

Last Flight, arranged by George Palmer Putnam. New York: Harcourt, Brace, 1937. An account of Amelia's ill-fated round-the-world flight consisting of her communications sent back along the way, arranged and edited by her husband.

20 Hrs. 40 Min.: Our Flight in the Friendship. New York: G. P. Putnam's, 1928. Amelia's story of her 1928 transatlantic flight.

Adult Biographies

Lovell, Mary S. *The Sound of Wings: The Life of Amelia Earhart.* New York: St. Martin's, 1989. A thorough, objective, beautifully written biography that credits the promotional activity of George Palmer Putnam with enabling Amelia to pursue a career in aviation.

Rich, Doris L. *Amelia Earhart: A Biography.* Washington: Smithsonian Institute Press, 1989. A popular, admiring biography, not favorably disposed toward Putnam.

Young-Adult Biographies

Lauber, Patrice. *Lost Star: The Story of Amelia Earhart*. New York: Scholastic, 1988. An objective account of Amelia's life and disappearance.

Pearce, Carol A. *Amelia Earhart*. New York: Facts On File, 1988. A well-balanced profile, with black-and-white photos and useful maps of Amelia's flights.

Randolph, Blythe. *Amelia Earhart*. New York: Franklin Watts, 1987. A frank, well-written biography that includes discussion of the various theories of Amelia's disappearance.

Sloate, Susan. *Amelia Earhart: Challenging the Skies*. New York: Fawcett, 1990. The most recent of many young-adult biographies, this volume stresses Amelia's feminism.

Edwin C. Musick

Ed Musick at the controls of a Sikorsky S-42 flying boat.
(Pan American World Airways)

*I*n October 1934, Juan Trippe, president of Pan American Airways, wrote a letter to the U.S. secretary of the navy informing him that Pan Am planned to establish air service between the United States and China by way of Hawaii, Midway, Wake, Guam, the Philippines, and Hong Kong. Trippe requested the navy's permission to use its facilities at Pearl Harbor and Manila and the islands of Midway, Wake (both uninhabited), and Guam, where Pan Am proposed to build marine airports for its flying boats. In the event of war, he promised, these bases would be turned over to the navy.

In 1934, Pan Am was America's only international airline and the only privately owned international airline in the world. But though privately owned, Pan Am had always had a close—indeed, dependent—relationship with the U.S. government. No airline at that time could exist without the airmail contracts awarded by the federal government. On the foundation of those lucrative airmail contracts, Pan Am in the 1920s had built a network of air routes from its base in Florida across the Caribbean and down the east coast of South America.

Successful in the Caribbean, Trippe aspired to develop air routes to both Europe and Asia. In 1931 and 1934 he sent Charles and Anne Lindbergh to survey, first, an Arctic route to the Far East and then a North Atlantic route to Europe. Trippe confidently ordered a fleet of large new flying boats in anticipation of getting those routes. When both routes were blocked, he audaciously determined to establish a route from California to China across the Pacific.

The difficulties of a Pacific air route were formidable. First, there were the great distances to be flown over water. From San Francisco to Honolulu was 2,400 miles; from Honolulu to Midway, 1,400; from Midway to Wake, 1,300; from Wake to Guam, 1,300; from Guam to Manila, 1,600; from Manila to Hong Kong, 700—a total of 8,700 miles. Yet in 1934 the longest distance regularly flown over water was 1,800 miles across the South Atlantic between Africa and Brazil, flown by French mail planes. The longest stretch of ocean that Pan Am flew in the Caribbean was 660 miles.

Then there was the problem of navigation. The Hawaiian Islands were small enough, but Midway, Wake, and Guam were mere specks in the vast Pacific. Under the best of circumstances, they were difficult to locate by the means of aerial navigation then available— and to miss them meant going down in the ocean. In the Pacific, there were no railroads, highways, or rivers that a pilot could follow. Dead reckoning alone—plotting speed, wind drift, and direction on a map—was too crude. Celestial navigation—using the sun or stars to find one's location—would be impossible in bad weather. The only way these islands could be located with any reliability was by radio navigation, which was then in its infancy.

Weather was yet another problem. Despite its name, the Pacific is a tempestuous area. The collision of polar and tropical air masses over its enormous expanse generates typhoons and hurricanes without warning. Wind patterns were uncharted. Weather stations were few. Unlike the Atlantic, the Pacific was plied by relatively few ships, and the amount of weather data that could be collected from them was insufficient to plot even the most rudimentary weather maps.

Finally, there was the problem of aircraft. In the early 1930s, all-metal airplanes were beginning to replace the wood-and-fabric craft of the 1920s. Their superior aerodynamic qualities and improved engines raised the revolutionary possibility of long-distance flying. But the fuel necessary to fly those distances would occupy most of the space on those planes. Could a plane be built with sufficient fuel and payload capacity to fly the Pacific profitably?

In 1931, Trippe drew up specifications for the kind of airplane he wanted—a four-engine flying boat with unprecedented speed, range, and load-carrying ability—and invited nine leading manufacturers to bid for contracts. Only two accepted the challenge— Igor Sikorsky and Glenn L. Martin; and in 1932 each was awarded a contract for three planes, to be delivered in 1934.

The Navy Department welcomed Trippe's letter. For many years, the navy had watched the growing power of Japan with alarm. From obscurity and isolation, Japan had rapidly emerged as a world power. It defeated China in 1895, Russia in 1905. It annexed Korea in 1910 and Manchuria in 1931. During World War I, Japan seized German-held islands in the western Pacific—the Marshalls, Carolines and Marianas. Under the terms of the League of Nations mandate by which Japan was permitted to keep those islands, she was forbidden to fortify them. But Japan sealed off the islands from foreigners, and suspicions grew that she was in fact building air and naval bases in the western Pacific. From these, she could cut U.S. communications with the Philippines (then a U.S. possession) or attack the U.S. naval base at Pearl Harbor in Hawaii.

The navy wanted bases of its own in the western Pacific, but it was prevented by treaty from fortifying the U.S. islands of Midway, Wake, and Guam. Thus the proposal from a commercial airline to build bases—for the use of civilian airplanes, of course, but readily convertible to military use—was very much in the national interest. The navy, with the assent of the State Department and the president, readily gave its permission for Pan Am to use its facilities and its islands, and thereafter it provided extensive logistical and personnel support.

In 1935, a freighter chartered by Pan Am carried supplies and personnel to Midway, Wake, and Guam. Diesel power plants, water and fuel storage tanks, radio and weather stations, roads and pipelines, machine shops, storehouses, office buildings and bungalows were built in preparation for the arrival of Pan Am airplanes on regular trips to and from the Far East. The next year hotels were built to accommodate Pan Am's passengers on their overnight stays on the islands.

Japan watched this activity with ill-concealed anger. Although its government remained silent, its newspapers were loud in their protests. The development of commercial aviation facilities on Midway, Wake, and Guam, declared Japanese editorial writers, was an obvious subterfuge. These, in fact, were military bases penetrating the island shield that guarded the Japanese homeland. In Washington, U.S. authorities became concerned that the Japanese might not be content with verbal protests.

By 1935 Trippe was ready to begin survey flights over the Pacific as far as Manila (the final leg of the journey, from Manila to Hong Kong, would not open until 1936). Survey flights would test Pan Am's new flying boats, train the flight crews and ground personnel, and gather information on weather and communication conditions in the Pacific. To direct these flights, Trippe assigned Pan Am's chief pilot, Edwin C. Musick.

Born in St. Louis on August 13, 1893, Ed Musick grew up in Los Angeles. In high school he was a popular athlete, but his great passions were automobiles and motorcycles. After graduation he went to work as an auto mechanic. His interest in aviation was aroused in 1910 at an air show in which pioneer "birdmen" exhibited their kitelike crates. Ed was impressed to learn that exhibition pilots could make $1,500 for a single performance.

With friends, Ed built two airplanes out of scrap material. Both crashed before getting off the ground. But the salvaged parts paid for Ed's first flying lessons. In 1914 he bought a used tractor biplane, taught himself stunt flying, and began appearing in carnivals as "Daredevil Musick." One night, while launching a fireworks display from his plane, he set the craft on fire. He brought the plane down seconds before it was consumed. Fire was the thing that pilots dreaded most, and landing his flaming plane that night marked the end of Musick's career as a stuntman. He would later say, "My idea is not to be the best pilot but the oldest."

When the United States entered World War I, Musick became a civilian flight instructor for the army in California and Texas. Later he was commissioned a lieutenant in the marines and sent to Miami as a flight instructor. When he left the marines in 1919, he worked for several short-lived airlines in Florida and New York. In the 1920s airplanes could not compete with trains for comfort and reliability over short distances.

Edwin C. Musick

In 1927 Pan Am hired Musick as its first pilot. On October 28 that year he inaugurated the company's mail service between Key West and Havana, flying a Fokker trimotor land plane. In succeeding years Pan Am extended its routes over the Caribbean and to South America. It switched from land planes to flying boats, adopting Sikorsky's twin-engine S-38. This was an awkward-looking plane, but it had surprising speed, range and payload.

As the airline expanded, so did Musick's role. His careful reports on problems of weather, navigation, communications, and landing facilities determined the company's procedures. He also hired and trained pilots and crews. The new pilots, former army and navy fliers, had to be taught that there was no place in commercial aviation for the high jinks they were accustomed to in the military. Safety was now the paramount concern, and courteous service to the civilian passengers a close second. Musick proved a strict disciplinarian, and his meticulous concern for the condition of the planes never relaxed.

Juan Trippe's decision to expand across the Atlantic and Pacific intensified pressure on the Pan Am crews based in Florida. Advanced new planes were on order, and to fly them over unprecedented ocean distances and in totally new conditions required highly trained crews. Musick recruited them from the Naval Reserve. Most of these young men were college graduates; all had trained at the navy's flying school at Pensacola and had at least 250 hours of flying time. They entered Pan Am's service as apprentice pilots, beginning in the radio and engineering departments before becoming junior pilots. When they were not flying, they were studying navigation, engineering and international law. Musick believed that his senior flying boat pilots should have the same maritime knowledge as the captain of an ocean liner. And in fact Musick established a shipboard nomenclature for his crews: the pilot was the captain, and under him served a first officer, a junior officer, an engineer, and stewards. All were addressed as "Mister," and all were outfitted in navy-like blue uniforms. For these new crews, the Caribbean became an aviation laboratory. Every flight was a training mission for the great tests that lay ahead.

In June 1934 the first of the new flying boats reached Pan Am's Miami base. It was a Sikorsky S-42. Shaped like a whale, it had a 114-foot wing with four 750-horsepower Hornet engines and new Hamilton Standard variable-pitch propellers. The array of new instruments in its cockpit caused Charles Lindbergh, head of Pan

Am's technical committee, to warn that the plane would need engineers as pilots. On test flights conducted by Lindbergh and Musick, the S-42 set new records for seaplane performance. Weighing 19 tons, it could fly 1,250 miles, with 32 passengers, a crew of five, and 2,500 pounds of mail, at 145 miles per hour. It had been built for the short distances of a transatlantic route—by way of either Greenland or the Azores—but it arrived after Trippe's bid for an Atlantic route had been blocked. Instead, the new plane was christened the *Brazilian Clipper* and assigned to the South America route.

To promote the *Brazilian Clipper*, Trippe in August 1934 hosted a party of newspaper publishers on a goodwill tour of South America. Musick piloted the S-42. There were overnight stops at San Juan, Puerto Rico; at Trinidad; and at Para and Natal in Brazil. While they were still an hour out of Rio de Janeiro, Musick learned that Rio's harbor was shrouded in fog. Although he was carrying his company's president and a group of influential passengers, and although a distinguished reception committee was waiting for them at Rio, Musick brought the clipper down onto a cove on the Atlantic coast. There the party spent the night before proceeding safely to Rio. The publishers continued on to Buenos Aires; from there Musick brought them back to Miami in five flying days—three days faster than previous trips.

It is evidence of Musick's authority that no one criticized his decision to avoid the fog at Rio. Musick had by then flown 10,000 hours and more than a million miles for Pan Am without an accident. His reputation for safety, for treating the most difficult flights as routine, was a major asset for the airline.

The Martin flying boats, intended for the long Pacific route, were behind schedule. Rather than delay the survey flights that must precede the start of Pan Am's Pacific service, Trippe ordered the Sikorsky flying boat pressed into service. The second Sikorsky clipper to reach Miami was sent back to the factory, where its interior furnishings were replaced by additional gas tanks that increased the plane's range to 3,000 miles. When it was returned to Miami, Musick and his crews put it to a month's intensive use, rehearsing the routines that would be used in flying the Pacific. In March 1935 Musick piloted the S-42 nonstop and overnight from Miami to the Virgin Islands and back again, a distance equivalent to that from San Francisco to Honolulu. On March 27 he flew the S-42 1,600 miles across the Gulf of Mexico and across

Mexico to Acapulco. The next day he flew it 1,400 miles to San Diego. On March 29, 20,000 people watched the flying boat descend onto San Francisco Bay and anchor at Pan Am's new marine airport at Alameda.

In California, Musick and his crew flew the S-42 day and night, learning every feature of the California coast, practicing night and blind flying, returning to Alameda from every point of the compasss. When at last they were ready to venture into the Pacific, it was decided to make a series of four survey flights, each one advancing one island base farther than the preceding one. This would permit Musick and his crew to absorb the lessons of each flight. It also enabled Trippe to make a publicity extravaganza of each.

At 3 P.M. on April 16, 1935, Musick took off from Alameda for Honolulu, 2,400 miles away. The S-42 landed at Pearl Harbor at 8 o'clock the next morning, exactly on schedule. Musick's flying time of 18 hours 37 minutes was six hours faster than the record, set just the year before. Four days later the S-42 returned to San Francisco. This time Musick fought head winds and crosswinds all the way, and for a time he was lost. The plane reached Alameda five hours late, its fuel almost exhausted. Musick ordered two additional months of practice flying in California. Not until June 12 did the S-42 take off again for Honolulu. This time, after a day's rest at Pearl Harbor, Musick proceeded 1,400 miles over the Pacific to Midway.

Musick's first officer, R. O. D. Sullivan, captained the S-42 on the flights to Wake in August and to Guam in October. Musick had been ordered to Baltimore to test fly the Martin M-130 flying boat, which had emerged from Glenn Martin's factory at Middle River, Maryland, a year behind schedule.

The M-130 represented a giant leap forward in aeronautical engineering. A third larger than the Sikorsky flying boat, it weighed 26 tons, had a wingspan of 130 feet, and was powered by four 800-horsepower Pratt & Whitney Wasp engines. Its streamlined, double-bottomed hull, 90 feet long, was divided into six watertight compartments, any two of which could keep the plane afloat if it was forced down on the ocean. Instead of wing pontoons like the S-42, it had stubby seawings, or sponsons, extending from the hull at the water line . These gave the plane increased stability on the surface and increased lift in flight.

The M-130 was the first aircraft capable of lifting its own weight in fuel and payload. Its lounge, three passenger cabins convertible into sleeping compartments, lavatory, and galley could accommodate 40 passengers (but only 10 or 11 on the Honolulu run, when additional fuel storage was needed). There were quarters for the crew in the tail. Fully loaded, the flying boat could cruse 3,200 miles nonstop at 156 miles per hour.

The China Clipper *being serviced during an overnight stopover along the transpacific route.*
(Pan American World Airways)

The first M-130 was named the *China Clipper*. Two later Martin flying boats, identical in outer appearance to the *China Clipper*, were named the *Philippine Clipper* and the *Hawaiian Clipper*. In the public's mind, all three became simply the *China Clipper*, the boldest, most beautiful, most glamorous aircraft of its day.

Musick tested the M-130 through the summer. On October 9 the big flying boat was formally transferred to Pan Am. After publicity flights over Washington and New York, Musick flew the *China Clipper* to Alameda by way of Miami, Acapulco, and San Diego. Juan Trippe wanted to inaugurate Pan Am's Pacific service as soon as possible. Although the Martin flying boat had never been flown in the Pacific and the winter storm season was approaching, Trippe selected November 22.

Edwin C. Musick

On November 22, 1935, 25,000 people gathered at Alameda to watch the *China Clipper* depart. From the San Francisco side of the bay, another 125,000 watched. The night before, agents of the Federal Bureau of Investigation had seized two Japanese nationals aboard the deserted clipper, apparently intent on sabotaging its radio direction finder, but this information was not made public. The day was brilliantly sunny, and the crowds were in a festive mood. After an hour of ceremonies, which were broadcast nationwide, Musick and a seven-man crew—two other pilots, a pilot-in-training, a navigator, two engineers, and a radio operator—boarded the clipper. There were no passengers, but the plane carried a ton of mail. At 3:45 P.M., Musick started up the plane's four engines, taxied out into the bay through crowds of small boats, and then, in a cloud of spray, lifted the big ship off the water, passed beneath the center span of the San Francisco–Oakland Bay Bridge, and headed out to sea.

Six days later, after 59 hours 48 minutes flying time, the *China Clipper* anchored at Manila, where 200,000 people cheered its arrival. A throng of newspaper reporters surrounded Musick, whose typically laconic comment was: "Without incident, an uneventful trip."

Musick brought the *China Clipper* back to Alameda on December 6. Meanwhile, on November 24, the second Martin flying boat, the *Philippine Clipper*, had arrived in Alameda from Baltimore. On December 9 another crew took the *Philippine Clipper* on the second flight to Manila, returning to California on December 26. Thereafter for two months the weather prevented both clippers from flying. Weather, however, was not the only problem. In January, during a break in the weather, Captain Sullivan was taxiing the *China Clipper* through the Alameda lagoon headed for San Francisco Bay and a flight to Honolulu when he hit a submerged object that ripped through the plane's hull. On the bottom of the lagoon, divers found concrete blocks from which iron rods protruded to within a few feet of the surface of the water. Again, Japanese sabotage was suspected, but the incident was covered up. Not until February 23 was Musick able to take off in the *China Clipper* for only the third trip to Manila.

In April, the arrival of the third Martin flying boat, the *Hawaiian Clipper*, together with the change of season, made possible the beginning of weekly flights across the Pacific. The clippers still carried only mail. In October the *China Clipper* carried its first passengers—a group of newspapermen—to Manila. A week later

Trippe escorted a party of business executives in the *Philippine Clipper* on the first flight to terminate in Hong Kong. Musick was the plane's captain on this trip. From San Francisco to Honolulu, only eight passengers could be accommodated because of the need for additional fuel tanks on the 2,400-mile flight. But seven more passengers, who had journeyed to Honolulu by steamer, joined the flight there and continued to Hong Kong. The first passenger flight open to the general public was scheduled for October 21. More than 1,200 people applied; only seven were accommodated.

By the end of 1936, Pan American clippers were making weekly passenger flights to the Far East. The great pioneering adventure had become routine—which was precisely what the company wanted. In 1937, however, Japan went to war with China. The clippers were now flying into a war zone, and the threat of Japanese interference was felt more keenly. In July 1938 the *Hawaiian Clipper* disappeared without warning or trace between Guam and Manila. Because one of its passengers was carrying a large sum of money destined for the Chinese government, the possibility of sabotage could not be dismissed. The cause of the disappearance was never discovered.

In addition to its interest in Midway, Wake, and Guam, the U.S. Navy had its eye on certain islands south and southwest of Hawaii that could prove useful in the defense of Hawaii and the Panama Canal, and that could also provide an alternative route to Australia and the Far East if Japan should seize Guam and cut off the mid-Pacific route. Again, the navy's interest and Pan Am's coincided. Juan Trippe saw a lucrative market in Australia, to be reached over a chain of tiny islands stretching south and west of Hawaii—Kingman Reef, Jarvis, Howland and Samoa. When he was barred from Australia because the United States would not permit British Imperial Airline to use Hawaii, he contented himself with Auckland, New Zealand as the terminus of his projected southern transpacific route.

In December 1937, Musick was detached from *China Clipper* service and assigned to survey this southern route. Since the three Martin flying boats were engaged elsewhere, he was given a Sikorsky S-42 equipped with long-distance fuel tanks and re-named the *Samoan Clipper*. On December 12, 1937, he left Alameda on his first survey flight over the southern route. From Alameda he piloted the *Samoan Clipper* to Honolulu, Kingman Reef, Samoa, and Auckland, then back to California. In January

The China Clipper *over San Francisco's Golden Gate Bridge (then under construction) on November 22, 1935.*
(Pan American World Airways)

1938 he set out to repeat the journey. This time, however, shortly after leaving Pago Pago on Samoa on January 11, the clipper's number-four engine developed an oil leak. Musick ordered the engine shut down and turned the clipper to return to Pago Pago.

Although the takeoff from Pago Pago was easy—straight out through the harbor entrance into prevailing head winds—the landing approach was difficult. The harbor was surrounded by steep mountains. An incoming seaplane had to skim the mountain tops, then dive for the harbor. In preparation for this tricky landing, Musick spent an hour burning off fuel before beginning the approach. Some 20 miles out of Pago Pago, flying at 10,000 feet, he jettisoned most of his remaining fuel. The gasoline sprayed out from dump valves on the underside of each wing, formed a vapor cloud around the plane, and then, ignited by the engine exhausts, exploded. The S-42 vanished in a fireball. The next day searchers found an oil slick and the debris of the wreck. Musick and his crew were dead. Musick, only 44 years old, the ever-cautious, safety-obsessed veteran pilot, had died in the way he feared most—by fire.

Soon after, Pan American abandoned its southern route.

In 1936 the International League of Aviators awarded Ed Musick its prestigious Harmon Trophy as "the world's outstanding aviator" of 1935 for his pioneering work establishing Pan American's clipper service across the Pacific. Only two Americans had won the Harmon Trophy before—Charles Lindbergh and round-the-world flier Wiley Post. Unlike Lindbergh and Post, Musick never made a spectacular flight. All his "first flights" were commercial surveys preparing Pan American's international routes in the Caribbean, South America, and finally the Pacific. The voluminous reports and opinions that Musick turned in to his superiors formed the basis for Pan American's final plans for its international airmail and passenger service.

"Musick's reports," the *New York Times* observed in reporting the pilot's death in the explosion of the *Samoan Clipper*, "indicated that he was more than an airplane pilot. He was an expert navigator, scientist, meteorologist and most of all an economist." The *Times* quoted a Pan Am official as saying, "Not a single impracticable suggestion was ever recommended by him."

Establishing international air routes was not a simple matter in the 1930s, when ground facilities and navigation aids were rudimentary or nonexistent, when little was known of wind patterns and weather conditions over large portions of the globe, and when the airplanes themselves were new and untried. With infinite care and discipline, Musick reduced deeds of extraordinary skill and daring to routine. That is what made international commercial aviation possible.

Chronology

August 13, 1893	born in St. Louis, Missouri
1910	sees first air show in Los Angeles, California, learns to fly

1917	serves as a civilian flight instructor for U.S. Army
1918	commissioned a lieutenant in the U.S. Marine Corps, serves as flight instructor
1919	begins period of freelance flying and employment with short-lived airlines
1927	becomes first pilot hired by Pan American Airways, inaugurates mail service between Key West, Florida, and Havana, Cuba
1934	pilots Pan American's *Brazilian Clipper* from Miami to Rio de Janeiro and back in record time
1935	directs Pacific survey flights for Pan American's *China Clipper* service between Alameda, California, and Manila, then pilots first trip by *China Clipper* (November 22–December 6)
1936	awarded Harmon Trophy as "world's outstanding aviator" of 1935 for his Pacific survey work for Pan American
1937	assigned to survey a southern transpacific route
January 11, 1938	dies at Pago Pago, Samoa, in explosion of *Samoan Clipper*

Further Reading

Bender, Marylin, and Selig Altschul. *The Chosen Instrument: Pan Am, Juan Trippe, and the Rise and Fall of an American Entrepreneur.* New York: Simon & Schuster, 1982. This biography of the founder and longtime president of Pan American Airways provides valuable information about the company's transpacific route and about Ed Musick's role.

Jackson, Ronald W. *China Clipper*. New York: Everest House, 1980. An account of the disappearance of the *Hawaiian Clipper* in 1938 affords an opportunity to relate the history of Pan Am's transpacific clipper service and of Musick's indispensable contributions.

Chuck Yeager

Chuck Yeager beside the X-1 rocket plane.
(Smithsonian Institution Photo No. A2013)

*T*wenty-one-year-old Second Lieutenant Chuck Yeager, U.S. Army Air Force, pulls himself out of his sleeping bag in the predawn darkness and stumbles out to the latrine, where he washes in cold water and shaves carefully (he will be wearing a close-fitting oxygen mask for six hours today). Back in the Nissen hut he shares with a dozen other pilots, he dresses, then bicycles to the briefing hut of the 357th Fighter Group, Eighth Air Force. The room is filled with half-awake men. There are briefings by the group leader, the intelligence officer, and the weather officer.

Dismissed, the men bike over to the operations shed. Yeager pulls on his flying suit, two pairs of woolen socks, fleece-lined boots. He straps on his .45, puts on his leather flying jacket and his Mae West, draws a parachute from supply, and finally puts on his leather flying helmet and goggles. Fully outfitted, he and the other pilots stand around in the brightening mist drinking coffee and eating dark bread spread with peanut butter and marmalade. There is little conversation. Finally, they climb aboard a weapons carrier and are driven out to the flight line, where their P-51 Mustangs stand ready.

It is October 12, 1944, on an airfield near Leiston, England. The field consists of three concrete runways in a sea of mud, rows of Nissen huts on one side, hangars and a control tower on the other. It is 60 miles north of London, only two miles from the North Sea. Across the water, Allied armies are fighting on German soil at Aachen and besieging Antwerp in Belgium. Every day and night, fleets of heavy bombers pass over the ground armies to hit targets deep in Germany. This day is like many others. Yeager's fighter group will fly cover for a formation of B-24 Liberator bombers on a daylight raid to Bremen, some 300 miles away.

Takeoff is at 8:00 A.M. The Mustangs, sleek and powerful, taxi by twos to the end of the runway, where an operations officer waves a red flag every eight seconds. The planes take off in pairs, one climbing straight ahead, the other turning briefly to take a parallel path. Although they are heavily loaded with ammunition and fuel—disposable wing tanks give the fighters a range of 2,000 miles—the planes' Rolls-Royce Merlin engines, generating 1,490 horsepower, lift them quickly from the runway. Landing gears are retracted. The planes climb through low-lying clouds, then pop out into dazzling sunlight. All three of the group's squadrons are assigned to this mission, each with four flights of four planes—a total of 48 planes. Although he is only a junior second lieutenant, Yeager is acting as group leader, a role usually filled by the group's commanding officer. But Yeager is a brilliant pilot, and he has phenomenal eyesight.

The planes circle briefly above the field, maneuvering into formation without radio contact. Then they turn east over the North Sea, climbing to 28,000 feet. Yeager's cockpit is not pressurized. He clips his oxygen mask in place. He feels the warm morning sun through the Plexiglas canopy. But it is 60 degrees below zero outside, and the lower half of his body is already cold and stiff. Yeager is in his element. He loves to fly, and he feels his plane as though it were an extension of himself. The best American fighter of the war, the Mustang can do 435 miles per hour in level flight. It is extremely maneuverable and deadly, with four machine guns. Its 2,000-mile range has transformed the nature of the air war by permitting fighters to accompany bombers on long-range missions. But the plane is vulnerable. There is a thick piece of armor at Yeager's back, but behind that is an 85-gallon tank of high-octane aviation gasoline. A bullet in the radiator could also prove fatal.

Over the Dutch coast, flak rises up and explodes in silent puffs around the fighters. A few minutes later they rendezvous with the B-24s. The bombers "chug along" at 200 miles per hour. The Mustangs, flying twice as fast, weave above them, on the lookout for Focke-Wulfs and Messerschmitts.

Yeager positions two squadrons to escort the bombers, then leads his own squadron to range 100 miles ahead. Over Germany he keeps a sharp eye on the sky above and behind him. The German that gets you, they say, is the one you never see. He checks his wingman, whose job it is to fly close beside and slightly to the rear as protection. Then he looks ahead, focusing on infinity and back, searching a section of sky every few seconds.

Over Steinhuder Lake, south of Bremen, Yeager sees specks in the sky 50 miles ahead. The Mustangs close fast. There are 22 Me-109s circling, waiting for the bombers. They don't see the American fighters coming toward them out of the sun. If they do, perhaps they mistake them for other 109s. They make no effort to get out of the way.

The Mustangs drop their wing tanks, then close to 1,000 yards, then 500. Yeager is in firing range of the rear plane in the German formation. Before he can fire, the German pilot spots him, swerves in alarm, and crashes into his own wingman. Both planes are destroyed.

Now the sky is filled with swirling, spinning, diving airplanes—16 Mustangs, 20 Messerschmitts. In a dogfight, the game is to get on the enemy's defenseless tail. Then it is a matter of anticipating his moves, outmaneuvering him, keeping him in your gunsights until you are within firing range. You try to come up at him from below, aiming ahead of him so your bullets will rip the length of his underside. It is not easy work. The Mustang's controls are not hydraulically operated, and at 400 miles an hour they become extremely heavy, while the G forces produced by diving and turning multiply the pilot's weight. In a dogfight, a pilot is soon sweating and breathing hard, his back and arms aching. The one who tires first will probably die.

The P-51 Mustang fighter of World War II.
(Smithsonian Institution Photo No. A2329B)

"I blew up a 109 from six hundred yards—my third victory," Yeager related of this dogfight, "—when I turned around and saw another angling in behind me. Man, I pulled back on my throttle so damned hard I nearly stalled, rolled up and over, and came in behind and under him, kicking right rudder and simultaneously firing. I was directly underneath the guy, less than fifty feet, and I opened up that 109 as if it were a can of Spam." Four victories. A moment later, he is on the tail of another 109. The German dives, Yeager pursues, firing. Yeager pulls out at 1,000 feet; the German goes into the ground. The fight breaks off. The Germans have lost eight planes, of which Yeager is credited with five. The Americans lose one.

The two fighter squadrons with the bombers, 50 miles away, hear the radio chatter of Yeager's squadron but they don't know where the fight is, and Yeager does not call them. Later, Yeager tells them, "There just weren't enough krauts to go around."

Chuck Yeager

The bombers fly unhindered to their target in Bremen. A cloud of smoke from previous bomber waves and from flak hangs over the city. While the Mustangs circle overhead, the bombers fly straight into the cloud on their target run. There is no evasive action. If one bomber is destroyed, ten crewmen die. The bombers emerge from the smoke into a clear sky and turn for home. Suddenly, 30 Messerschmitts attack. The Mustangs dive into the German formation. They shoot down eight, losing three of their own.

The flight home seems interminable. It is early afternoon over the North Sea when the bombers part company with their escort. Yeager drops to 3,500 feet and unfastens his oxygen mask. He is tired and hungry, and he has a headache. The cockpit smells of gas, oil and sweat. He gnaws at a hard D-ration chocolate bar. The control tower at Leiston gives him a compass reading, and the fighters head for the base. One by one they circle the field and swoop down to land, then taxi to the hardstand where the ground crews are waiting. There is an hour of debriefing with the intelligence officer before the pilots are freed for the rest of the day.

Tomorrow will probably be the same.

Charles E. Yeager was born on February 13, 1923, in Myra, West Virginia, a tiny Appalachian community on the Mud River consisting of a few farmhouses, a post office, and a general store. He was the second of five children of hardscrabble but self-sufficient mountain people. When he was a preschooler, the family moved down the river to Hamlin, a town of 400 inhabitants. His father was away from home all week working as a driller in natural gas fields. His mother raised five children, took care of a cow, pigs and chickens, cooked, mended and cleaned. The work was never done, and from an early age the children had their chores to do. But in summer they ran barefoot and hunted and fished. Chuck also became familiar with automobile and pump engines. He was a natural mechanic, with endless curiosity about how machinery worked.

Chuck graduated from Hamlin High School in 1941. There was no thought of college. Instead, at age 18, he enlisted in the Army Air Force and was trained as an airplane mechanic. In December 1941 the United States entered World War II, and Chuck's two-year enlistment was extended "for the duration." In 1942 he applied for a "flying sergeant" program. There were few enlisted men in his primary flying school; most of the cadets were college men who would be commissioned second lieutenants when they got their wings. Sensitive about his modest education, but competitive and aggressive, Yeager worried how he would stack up against the college boys. He proved to be a natural pilot, skilled and daring. When he graduated, he was made a flight officer—a noncommissioned rank that entitled him to wear an officer's uniform but with blue shoulder bars instead of the gold bars of a lieutenant. Selected for training as a fighter pilot, he reported to the 363rd Fighter Squadron, which trained for six months in Nevada, California, and Wyoming. In November 1943 the squadron arrived in England, where it joined the 357th Fighter Group at Leiston.

Yeager's squadron first saw action in February 1944. He had completed eight missions, and had shot down one German plane, when, on March 5, 1944, he was himself shot down over German-occupied France. Rescued by the French underground, he was escorted south to the Pyrenees, which he crossed on foot into Spain. He returned to England in May 1944. Air force policy was to return "evadees" to the States for fear that, if they fell into German hands, they might divulge information about the French resistance. Yeager was determined not to go home to an ignominious job training other pilots. He appealed the regulation up the chain of command. General Dwight D. Eisenhower eventually made the decision that kept Yeager with his fighter group.

During the next seven months, Yeager completed a total of 61 combat missions, during which he scored 12 victories. His last mission was on January 15, 1945. Of the 30 men in his original squadron who had trained and fought together, 13 had been killed and eight were missing in action. Only nine survived. Yeager went home with the rank of captain and a chestful of decorations. He was just 22.

Former evadees had the privilege of choosing their next post. Yeager chose Wright Field in Dayton, Ohio, because it was near Hamlin, and he reported there in July 1945. He was luckier than he knew. Wright Field was the center for air force testing and development. As assistant maintenance officer in the fighter test section, Yeager was able to fly all the planes at the field, including captured German and Japanese fighters, the Bell P-59 (the prototype U.S. jet fighter), and the Lockheed P-80 Shooting Star, the first operational U.S. jet fighter. For a country boy who wanted nothing more than to fly, Wright Field was "hog heaven." He flew six to eight hours a day, checking out 25 different planes. When he first took the controls of the Shooting Star, he was astonished. Cruising straight and level, he flew at 550 miles per hour, faster than he had in a full-throttle power dive in a Mustang. "I felt like I was flying for the first time," he recalled.

As a lowly maintenance officer, Yeager was hardly in the same league with the test pilots at Wright Field, all of whom were college graduates, most with engineering degrees. They looked down their noses at the fighter jock with the hillbilly accent, and they were not amused when he flew rings around them in mock dogfights and dazzled air-show audiences with his aerobatics. His aggressive, brilliant flying was noticed by his commanding officer, however. In short order, Yeager was assigned to a six-month course for test pilots, learning to fly in extremely precise patterns and to record flight data for the evaluation of airplanes. A few months later, to the outrage of the experienced test pilots, he was selected to be the principal test pilot for a totally new airplane, the Bell X-1, an experimental rocket plane designed to break the sound barrier.

The sound barrier was the big obstacle to the further development of aviation. No one knew what would happen when a plane reached Mach 1, the speed of sound—760 miles per hour at sea level. Judging from the buffeting of shock waves that planes experienced as they approached Mach 1, there was reason to fear that the sound barrier was like an invisible brick wall in the sky, against which a plane would hurtle to its destruction. It was necessary to find out, and the X-1 was designed for the job.

The X-1 was a small ship, 31 feet long with a wingspan of 28 feet. Its straight wings were extremely thin to minimize shock waves. Its tail was high to escape the turbulence coming off the wings. But this beautiful and delicate-looking plane was built to withstand 18 times the force of gravity. It was powered by four rocket engines fueled by liquid oxygen and alcohol. The plane could not take off from the ground, but had to be carried aloft by a B-29 Superfortress and dropped like a bomb. And it was in fact a flying bomb. Every inch of space in its sleek fuselage was devoted to the storage of its explosive fuel.

In July 1947 Yeager reported to the huge Muroc (later Edwards) Air Force Base in California's Mojave Desert. The scientists and engineers of the National Advisory Committee for Aeronautics (NACA), forerunner of the space agency, had expected a senior test pilot–engineer; instead they got a very junior 24-year-old captain with a high school diploma. The rumor was that the air force considered him expendable.

Flights in the X-1 started in August. There were three familiarization flights, without fuel. The plane was dropped from the B-29 at 25,000 feet, and Yeager glided it down to the dry lakebed. Even on later powered flights he would make dead-stick (unpowered) landings. Any fuel that was not consumed in flight had to be jettisoned before landing because of its volatility.

Powered flights began on August 29. The program called for two flights a week, each of only a few minutes' duration, approaching Mach 1 by small increments. The X-1 carried 500 pounds of monitoring instruments, and the NACA scientists wanted to analyze the data for each flight before proceeding with the next. Yeager's first powered flight reached .85 Mach. Gradually, speeds increased. On the seventh flight, at .94 Mach, Yeager discovered he had no pitch control. A shock wave on the tail's elevator immobilized it. For a few days it appeared that the program had reached a dead end. But the plane's designers had anticipated the loss of elevator effectiveness and had built in limited movement in the horizontal stabilizer, the portion of the tail in front of the elevator. That limited movement sufficed to keep the X-1 flying.

Yeager's ninth flight, on October 14, was planned to reach .97 Mach. He climbed aboard the B-29 mother ship around 8:00 A.M. The X-1 was already loaded. It had been backed into a cross-shaped pit and the B-29 pulled over it. Then it had been hoisted up and hooked to the B-29's bomb bay with a bomb shackle. Yeager sat on a box in the bomber's cockpit behind the pilot while the heavily loaded plane taxied and took off.

The B-29 climbed slowly. At 12,000 feet Yeager went back to the open bomb bay, climbed down a ladder through the roaring slipstream, and slid feet first through an opening in the top of the X-1 into its cabin. Unknown to his superiors, the night before he had broken two ribs in a fall from a horse. The ribs were taped now, but movement of any kind was intensely painful. He had stored a broom handle in the X-1's cabin, and now he used it to raise the overhead door into locking position with minimum movement of his arms. After that, there was little occasion for physical movement in the X-1's tiny cabin. Yeager sat on his parachute. Because the cockpit floor sloped upward, his knees were higher than his shoulders. His feet rested on rudder pedals. All the instrument switches were on the H-shaped control wheel.

Yeager put on his helmet and oxygen mask and hooked into the bomber's communication system. Then he waited while the bomber continued to climb at 180 miles per hour. The cabin was frigid. In the compartment directly behind him were stored hundreds of gallons of liquid oxygen at 296 degrees below zero. At 20,000 feet the bomber began a shallow dive to pick up speed. The loaded X-1 would stall at anything below 240 miles per hour. When the bomber reached that speed its pilot alerted Yeager and began to count backward from ten. At the count of one, there was a loud crack as the bomb shackle released the X-1. The X-1 dropped free of the B-29, falling out of the dark bomb bay into brilliant sunlight.

The X-1 suspended from a B-29 in flight.
(Smithsonian Institution Photo No. 83-2452)

The bomber had been flying too slow, and the X-1 fell in a nose-up stall. For a few seconds Yeager struggled to get the nose down while the rocket plane dropped toward the desert. When the plane was level, he switched on all four rocket chambers in rapid sequence. With a roar, the X-1 streaked up into the dark blue sky, slamming Yeager back in his seat. He climbed at .88 Mach in eerie quiet, the X-1 outracing the noise of its rockets. Yeager could hear his own breathing in his oxygen mask.

At 36,000 feet Yeager turned off two rocket chambers. At 40,000 feet he was still climbing at .92 Mach. At 42,000 feet he leveled off. With a third of his fuel still left, he turned on another rocket. The plane shot ahead—.96 Mach, .965 Mach. With the horizontal stabilizer providing pitch control, the X-1 hurtled through the sky. The faster it went, the smoother it flew. The Mach needle fluttered, then tipped off the scale. Yeager was flying faster than sound, at 1.07 Mach. There was no brick wall in the sky after all. Below on the desert floor the NACA scientists heard a distant rumble of thunder—the first sonic boom.

The breaking of the sound barrier was kept a military secret for several months. When at last it became public knowledge, Yeager went to Washington, met the president, Defense Department officials, and senators and congressmen, receiving another Distinguished Flying Cross and numerous trophies and plaques. Thereafter, the amiable hero was sent off as an air force spokesman to address civilian audiences around the country. But he was not permitted to profit in any way from his celebrity, and it was seven more years before he was promoted to major.

Yeager remained in the supersonic flight test program at Edwards Air Force Base until 1954, establishing new records and winning new honors. Then he resumed a more conventional air force career. Promoted to major, he commanded a fighter jet squadron in Europe in 1954–57, attended the Air War College, and served as head of the Air Force Aerospace Research Pilots School, a short-lived air force project for training military astronauts. In 1966 he was promoted to colonel and assigned as a wing commander to Vietnam and then Korea. He became a one-star general in 1968, serving as vice commander of the 17th Air Force in Germany in 1968–70 and as U.S. Defense Representative to Pakistan in 1971–72. He retired from active service in 1975.

The aeronautical data that Yeager and his fellow test pilots collected at Muroc from flights of the X-1 and new jet planes made possible the era of supersonic flight. Today speeds in excess of Mach 2—twice the speed of sound—are routine for military fighters and for the world's only supersonic commercial airliner, the Concorde. Economics alone prevents the development of more and faster supersonic airplanes.

Yeager's passing from the aviation scene marked the end of a chapter in aviation history. He was the last of the hero aviators—the men and women whose names are associated in the public mind with landmark achievements in flight. The breaking of the sound barrier inevitably recalls that very first breaking of the bonds that held humans fast to the earth, when, only 44 years before, the Wright brothers launched their fragile ship from the sands of Kitty Hawk—and flew.

Chronology

February 13, 1923	born in Myra, West Virginia
1941	graduates from high school in Hamlin, West Virginia, enlists in the U.S. Army Air Force as aviation mechanic
1942	accepted for flight training in "flying sergeant" program
1943	commissioned flight officer, trains as fighter pilot, goes to England with 363rd Fighter Squadron
1944	shot down over occupied France, returns to England via Spain, resumes tour of duty in which he flies 61 combat missions, scores 12 victories
1945	returns to United States, assigned to Wright Field, Dayton, Ohio
1946	trains as test pilot
1947	breaks sound barrier in rocket-powered Bell X-1 (October 14)
1954	promoted to major, commands fighter squadron in Europe
1961	graduates from Air War College
1962	heads Air Force Aerospace Research Pilots School

1966	promoted to colonel, serves as wing commander in Vietnam and Korea
1968	promoted to brigadier general, serves as vice commander, 17th Air Force in Germany
1971	appointed U.S. Defense Representative to Pakistan
1975	retires from air force

Further Reading

Books by Chuck Yeager

Yeager, General Chuck, and Leo Janos. *Yeager: An Autobiography*. New York: Bantam, 1985. A racy autobiography that provides vivid accounts of the experiences of a fighter pilot and test pilot. His wife and friends add their own comments to Yeager's narrative.

Yeager, General Chuck, and Charles Leerhsen. *Press On! Further Adventures in the Good Life*. New York: Bantam, 1988. Reflections on Yeager's childhood, flying, and the outdoor life, enlivened by comments from friends.

Index

Boldface numbers indicate main headings.

Index

Index

119

Index

Index

Index